CHOSEN *to be* GOD'S PROPHET

CHOSEN *to be* GOD'S PROPHET

HOW GOD WORKS IN *and* THROUGH THOSE HE CHOOSES

HENRY BLACKABY

OLIVER
NELSON
™

THOMAS NELSON PUBLISHERS®
Nashville

A Division of Thomas Nelson, Inc.
www.ThomasNelson.com

Published in Nashville, Tennessee, by Thomas Nelson, Inc.

Unless otherwise noted, Scripture quotations are from THE NEW KING JAMES VERSION. Copyright © 1979, 1980, 1982, Thomas Nelson, Inc., Publishers.

Scripture quotations noted KJV are from the KING JAMES VERSION of the Holy Bible.

Published in association with the literary agency of Wolgemuth & Associates, Inc.

Library of Congress Cataloging-in-Publication Data

Blackaby, Henry T., 1935-
    Chosen to be God's prophet : how God works in and through those he chooses / Henry Blackaby.
        p. cm.
    Includes bibliographical references.
    ISBN 0-7852-6555-4 (HC)
    ISBN 0-7852-6216-4 (IE)
    1. Samuel (Biblical judge) 2. Clergy—Religious life. I. Title.
    BS580.S2 B57 2003
    222'.43092—dc21   2002015692

Printed in the United States of America

03 04 05 06 07 BVG 6 5 4 3 2 1

To the many spiritual leaders who earnestly desire to be true to their call and the sacred covenant to which they have been called. I speak and pray with them constantly and know the depth of their hearts for God.

CONTENTS

CONTENTS

INTRODUCTION

SAMUEL

CRISIS! CRISIS IN THE MIDST OF GOD'S PEOPLE! What does God do when there is crisis among His people? The two books of 1 and 2 Samuel are classic expressions of the heart of God in times of spiritual and physical crises among His covenant people. God had entered into a covenant with His people. This covenant process is first seen in Exodus 19 and 20. Then God expands specifically, and in great detail, the conditions of this covenant in what we know as the Law. But essentially the Law was to be for their relationship with Him. He was not there for them; they were to be there for Him. Listen to the clear and simple statements of God to His people (from Exodus 19):

> ". . . and brought you [out of Egyptian bondage] to Myself" (v. 4).
>
> ". . . you shall be a special treasure to Me above all people" (v. 5).
>
> ". . . you shall be to Me a kingdom of priests" (v. 6).
>
> "And you shall be to Me . . . a holy nation" (v. 6).

The one clear and simple condition that His now-chosen people were asked to meet: "Obey My voice and keep My covenant" (Ex. 19:5). Throughout the rest of the Old and New Testaments, crises nearly always were seen when His people departed from their covenant relationship with God, as stated here and detailed later.

Since "covenant" is so crucial to understanding the relationship between God and His people, we would do well to take a moment now to explain this further.

A covenant with God had several significant features:

1. It was always a choice God made! It was initiated by Him and for His eternal purposes in the world.

2. His choice of a people was not based on the people, but on His love. This is clearly seen in Deuteronomy 7:6–11:

For you are a holy people to the LORD your God; the LORD your God has chosen you to be a people for Himself, a special treasure above all the peoples on the face of the earth. The LORD did not set His love on you nor choose you because you were more in number than any other people, for you were the least of all peoples; but because the LORD loves you, and because He would keep the oath which He swore to your fathers, the LORD has brought you out with a mighty hand, and redeemed you from the house of bondage, from the hand of Pharaoh king of Egypt. Therefore know that the LORD your God, He is God, the faithful God who keeps covenant and mercy for a thousand generations with those who love Him and keep His commandments; and He repays those who hate Him to their face, to destroy them. He will not be slack with him who hates Him; He will repay him to his face. Therefore you shall keep the commandments, the statutes, and the judgments which I command you today, to observe them.

This is stated further in Deuteronomy 10:12–13: "And now, Israel, what does the LORD your God require of you, but to fear the LORD your God, to walk in all His ways and to love Him, to serve the LORD your God with all your heart and with all your soul, and to keep the commandments of the LORD and His statutes which I command you today for your good?"

But, we also must remember this same truth is stated by Jesus to His disciples in John 15:16: "You did not choose Me, but I chose you and appointed you that you should go and bear fruit, and that your fruit should remain, that whatever you ask the Father in My name He may give you."

3. God spelled out very clearly the conditions that were to be followed by His covenant people. He promised to be faithful to them completely and to bless them above all the peoples of the earth (Ex. 19:5). They were to fear Him, love Him, obey Him, and serve Him, keeping all His commandments (Deut. 10:12–13). If they did not obey Him, He would discipline them and work against them. The most complete and detailed description of these two sides to God's relationship with His people can be seen and read in Deuteronomy 28.

4. When God's people lived faithfully with God, God would bless all the nations of the world through them. This is still true today. Jesus stated this clearly in Matthew 28:18–20. We would do well to remember that the most crucial aspect of God's covenant with His people, in both the Old Testament and the New Testament, was that His people were to be faithfully and constantly taught "to observe [practice and live out faithfully] all things that I have commanded you" (Matt. 28:20; see also Deut. 30:15–20).

5. As the people obeyed, God promised, "And lo, I am with you always, even to the end of the age" (Matt. 28:20; see also Deut. 32:46–47).

What an extensive promise of God! What a privilege for anyone to be chosen of God to be His people in a covenant relationship with Him! You may want to reflect on how Jesus saw this with His disciples in John 17.

Unfortunately, the heart of the people of God tended constantly to depart from their covenant relationship with Him, and the result was that God sought to bring them back to Himself. He would call for His people to "turn and live!" (Ezek. 18:32; see also Zech. 1:3; Mal. 3:7). Throughout the Bible the word *repent* is nearly always a call to God's people to return to their relationship with Him. This is the final cry of God in the book of Revelation as He was speaking to the seven churches of Asia Minor. Repentance was at the heart of the preaching of John the Baptist and also of the preaching of Jesus in the Gospels. God is constantly calling His people to repent or turn from their sin and rebellion, and again experience the fullness of His covenant. This call to repentance for God's people must always remain the heart of the preaching and teaching of the churches today. A lost world depends on the vital relationship of the people of God with their God. To lose this closeness with God is to lose our significance in our world.

Because of God's covenant with His people, when they departed God would raise up a prophet, a spiritual leader, to call His people back to Him.

All through Biblical history God has raised up for Himself (1 Sam. 2:35) individuals to minister to His people. Noah, Abraham, Joshua, Nathan, Isaiah, Jeremiah, Ezekiel, and many others were sent by God to teach His people, "This is the way, walk in it" (Isa. 30:21).

Even after Biblical times, throughout history God has continued to raise up individuals to minister to His people. For example, when God's people no longer believed that God answered prayer, God caused George Mueller to have a burden for the people of God to once again know that God responds to the prayers of His people. And history has shown that God did used George Mueller to turn the hearts of His people to once again pray believing. The world has come to hear the gospel, because God's people prayed.

In my own life, God placed me right in the middle of crisis of the people of God. In Canada during the 1960s, God's people at Faith Baptist Church had two pastors who stayed a very short time. The church remained without a pastor for several years. Their hearts became weary, and they began to move to disband the church.

The almost one million people of the province, and 135,000 people of the city, needed desperately to hear the gospel. But God's covenant people were in a spiritual crisis, and they no longer believed God could help them.

At such a time of crisis, what was on the heart of God for their future? What did He do for them? He put it on their hearts to know of my availability to consider their cry. God did a strong work in my life to show me He wanted to use this covenant people for a great work, even to participate in a real revival.

God put us together, and over the next twelve years God renewed these ten remaining people in the congregation, began thirty-eight new congregations through them, brought the "Canadian Revival" to their city, called over one hundred people into ministry, started a theological school to train the ones He was calling, and sent many across the nation and the world to serve Him.

God saw the crisis, raised up a servant for Himself, and led His people back into a vital relationship with Him. I was there! I was the one God raised up and sent to His people. God kept His covenant with His people.

He is still doing this wherever His people remember and understand God, His covenant, and His ways.

In our day, God continues to be faithful to His covenant by raising up those that He can use to help His people!

We, too, are the covenant people of God in our day. God will be working clearly and thoroughly in us, in every moment of crisis. Whether that moment is personal, in our families, in our local churches, or even in a denomination or ministry group, God remains the same. His ways are always the same. The method He chooses to implement His ways may differ from situation to situation, but God Himself remains the same. This book will explore, from the heart of God, what He does in the midst of His people in times of crises. Seeing and understanding the ways of God is crucial for every believer and every church. So as you study with me the working of God in the midst of His people through a person of His choosing—Samuel—we will pause regularly to check and see if our lives or the lives of our churches need adjusting to God. We must see if God, in love, is working clearly and thoroughly with us. If not, we must then seek together, by the Holy Spirit's enabling, to return fully to our covenant relationship with God, so He can redeem a lost world through us, His people, in our generation.

The covenant relationship we have with God is lived out in the midst of what I call *defining moments*. These are specific moments in the lives of God's people when they have to make decisions in their relationships with God. A covenant people's life depends on the quality of their relationship with God. Their decisions will always reveal their relationships with God! The reference point, or standard, God always uses is His stated covenant. God's covenant was written down; they read it constantly and were to live by it faithfully and diligently.

Today, every believer is in a *new* covenant with God—through Christ's blood (see Luke 22:20; 1 Cor. 11:25). Hear what Jesus said: "Likewise He also took the cup after supper, saying, "This cup is the new covenant in My blood, which is shed for you" (Luke 22:20). This is a real and dyamic covenant. The Scriptures, especially the Gospels, reveal to us the covenant's conditions. We are to diligently read the words of this covenant and follow them faithfully. For instance, Jesus said that every believer was to be taught to "observe [practice, live out in their lives] all things that I have commanded you" (Matt. 28:20). The church in the early chapters of Acts did exactly this, and God brought their entire world to hear the gospel through them. But every succeeding generation of God's people must also be taught, or their hearts (first love) will depart and God's eternal purpose through His people will be hindered.

This is also our solemn responsibility today. The study of the life of Samuel will help us see God clearly and respond to Him in our day. This study is not merely a review of the historical life of Samuel. Rather, it is a fresh look at God, His nature, His ways, and His heart. This book is designed to help us know more of Him and respond to Him in our lives and churches. We will seek to constantly apply what we read from Scriptures to our lives! Without applying the truths of God in His Word, it is all dead! James urged this in his letter to the believers in the early church by saying:

> But do you want to know, O foolish man, that faith without works is dead? Was not Abraham our father justified by works when he offered Isaac his son on the altar? Do you see that faith was working together with his works, and by works faith was made perfect? And the Scripture was fulfilled which says, "Abraham believed God, and it was accounted to him for righteousness." And he was called the friend of God. You see then that a man is justified by works, and not by faith only. (James 2:20–24)

Further, you will see the progressive activity of God with His people. He builds on what He does, so He can move His servant and His people in the midst of His eternal purposes. The life of Samuel is one picture in time—but a very important one. May God's Spirit guide us in our study and application of the Word to our lives.

SECTION

I

A FAITHFUL PRIEST

*Then I will raise up for Myself a faithful priest who shall do
according to what is in My heart and in My mind.
I will build him a sure house, and he shall walk
before My anointed forever.*

1 SAMUEL 2:35

ONE

DEFINING MOMENTS IN SAMUEL'S LIFE

In those days there was no king in Israel;
everyone did what was right in his own eyes.

Judges 17:6

WHEN YOU READ ABOUT THE LIFE of Samuel there are incredible defining moments that capture your attention. Many events that happen throughout an ordinary day are not noteworthy. There are all kinds of routines that are normal and natural every day. But *defining moments* of life shape the whole direction in which you go. These moments may determine where you live, who you marry, what college you attend, or what direction your occupation takes. As these defining moments come, they bring both soberness and joy to life.

> **Defining moments of life shape the whole direction in which you go.**

Reading and meditating on Samuel's defining moments will help you take a closer look at your own life. If you will take a spiritual inventory of your life, ministry, and family, you will find there are some moments that are different from the run-of-the-mill moments. These moments are so incredibly different from the ordinary times of life that you simply cannot forget what God did in your life, to your life, and through your life. These defining moments that come in your relationship to God, your ministry, or your life itself then shape and define your life.

This book will seek to share from the Scriptures how God worked in and through a man called Samuel. Yet you must not study and observe Samuel's life without taking time to make adjustments in your own life, especially with God! When you read of how God directed Samuel, you will become aware that there is a clear word from the Scriptures for your own life also. For Samuel, God guided and shaped him to be a prophet in the midst of His people when the people insisted on disobeying Him.

National and local occurrences in our day can also be defined as times of spiritual crisis, as occurred in Samuel's day. But what are the dynamics involved in crucial times? What does God have in mind when He selects and shapes a person? How does He go about it? How does He bring His purposes to pass through His chosen servant? A glimpse into what God did in Samuel will help you see what God must do to develop the leader His people need. In turn, this will help you define God's divine moments in your life.

GOD'S INITIATIVE . . . NOT OURS

The common people of this generation are not looking for professional religionists to find real answers. Professional religionists often are what turn the common person away from God. People want a deep, abiding, and real relationship with God. Yet on our own, within that relationship, every one of us can have down times and even question our calls. None of us will, at times, be immune from looking over our lives and questioning why nothing seems to be happening. We can become very self-centered. But when God chooses someone, He Himself will affirm that person before the eyes of all the people.

Would you rather try to endorse your own ministry before people or would you rather have God endorse and affirm you? You do not confirm your ministry, God does! If He does not, you are in trouble. You can launch a public-relations campaign so you will be more acceptable. However, seeking acceptance from the world is of no use to God. You do not have to announce you are going to have a big building program and then blame the people if it does not work. If God wants a building program, it will work. If you start something and it does not seem to go well, consider carefully that God, on purpose, may not be authenticating what you told the people—because it did not come from Him, but from your own head. You may have wanted to do something outstanding for God and forgot that God does not want that. He wants you to be available to Him, and more important, to be obedient to Him. God is looking for a person in whom He can entrust His leadership. The key is not what a person can do, but what God will do in and through a person's life.

We will not be looking so much at Samuel as at the God who called Samuel. We will examine what God does in a time of crisis. It is critical to understand that the time of Samuel's calling fell during the worst era in Israel's history. Four hundred years of the judges had brought them to this time. Sadly, it was a time very similar to our own as we also see what the Scripture says: "Everyone did what was right in his own eyes" (Judg. 21:25).

> **You do not confirm your ministry, God does!**

The culture of 1960s absolutely captured many of God's people so that they did what was right in their own eyes. God's children began to want to find "their gift" and "their ministry" and go off and do it regardless of the impact it had on anyone else. Spiritual anarchy became the defining moment of those days. Christians forgot they were a covenant people. They forgot they were part of a corporate call of God.

But God called Christians to be a holy nation. They are to corporately function together. The darkest times of Samuel's day revealed that the people of God would do what was right in their own eyes. Into that critical time God called a servant, the first of the prophets—Samuel.

In a dream to Abimelech, God called Abraham a prophet (see Gen. 20:7). But here we are seeing Samuel as the first of a long line of prophets. And so he is unique. I sense that the Christians of our day need not just preachers; they need a special kind of spokesman for God. Put the name "prophet" over him if you want.

A major part of the tragedy of this four-hundred-year period is that the leaders of the people of God never recognized that they were in a deep problem. They never recognized that they themselves were the problem. Godless thinking, especially by the leaders, put the people into four hundred years of spiritual bondage.

You have to go back to Judges chapter 2 to see the pain of the situation. To what can you attribute the problem? Is there any clue here?

I had to face this passage as a young boy, as a teenager, as a young man, then when I was in seminary, and in the first churches that I pastored. I thank God that He made me process it in my own ministry. Maybe it was because I had been a history major and had studied so much of what had happened in previous generations. If any generation refuses to study history, they are doomed to repeat it. Every generation, including ours, is preeminently tied to the activity of God in those who preceded them. "When all that generation had been gathered to their fathers, another generation arose after them who did not know the LORD nor the work which He had done for Israel" (Judg. 2:10).

KNOW THE GOD OF YOUR FATHERS

There arose on the scene of the people of God a younger generation that felt they had to begin everything new without any reference to what God had done for Israel. They could not, and would not, recite any of the mighty acts of God done in other generations. Therefore, they did not know the God of their fathers. They had no reference point to the God who delivered the children of Israel out of Egypt. They hardly remembered the stories. They did not understand at all the time in the wilderness. They did not know the mighty deeds of God at Jericho. This generation determined that anything they labeled tradition was to be turned aside. Was it possible that the previous generation, who did know God, failed to adequately instruct the next generation?

In our own generation, what many today are calling *tradition* is really the mighty acts of God, which He has done in His people. No child of God must ever forget what God has done. If he does, he will not be able to build on what God has done previously. If you try to lay another foundation than that which has already been laid by God, He will let you. The cost of missing what God has already done will be great as you attempt to move forward in your own decisions. Understand, though, that to ignore what God has already done is disobedience. You can call it "creative ministry" all you want, but God may simply call it disobedience.

You are not to ignore the God of your fathers. You are to ask the older generation to tell you what God did in your community to start the church you are now attending. What did God do when He brought that group of people together to begin His local church in that area? Do not try to live in your

> **You are not to ignore the God of your fathers.**

generation as though you have nothing to do with the previous generation. You are a vital part of a covenant people of God. If all you see that has gone before you are men and you say, "They had their time; now we have our turn," you do not understand that it was not them who built the church; it was God! Do not confuse the men who have preceded you with the God who has preceded you. God later instructed Jeremiah to tell the people:

> Thus says the LORD:
> "Stand in the ways and see,
> And ask for the old paths, where the good way is,
> And walk in it;

Then you will find rest for your souls.

But they said, 'We will not walk in it.'" (Jer. 6:16)

When I hear some people disparage the older generation, I do not hear them make any reference to God. It is as though they are saying, "Now that I am on the scene, God has come." But long before God called me, He was working in the hearts of those who laid down their lives to follow Him. They heard a call from God, and they did all they knew to do. They knew another generation would arise after them. The cry of their hearts was, "Oh, that they would understand the mighty deeds of God." Many of the newer generations, however, forgot the works of God because the older generation never taught or impressed on their minds all His wonderful deeds.

Such was the case in Eli's life. Eli lost his two sons. They became of no use to God because Eli would not teach them the things of God. God indicted Eli, who said he was far more concerned about his sons than he was about God. God then pronounced judgment and stated that both Eli and his two sons would die.

> Then a man of God came to Eli and said to him, "Thus says the LORD: 'Did I not clearly reveal Myself to the house of your father when they were in Egypt in Pharaoh's house? Did I not choose him out of all the tribes of Israel to be My priest, to offer upon My altar, to burn incense, and to wear an ephod before Me? And did I not give to the house of your father all the offerings of the children of Israel made by fire? Why do you kick at My sacrifice and My offering which I have commanded in My dwelling place, and honor your sons more than Me, to make yourselves fat with the best of all the offerings of Israel My people?' Therefore the LORD God of Israel says: 'I said indeed that your house and the house of your father would walk before Me forever.' But now the LORD says: 'Far be it from Me; for those who honor Me I will honor, and those who despise Me shall be lightly esteemed. Behold, the days are coming that I will cut off your arm and the

arm of your father's house, so that there will not be an old man in your house. And you will see an enemy in My dwelling place, despite all the good which God does for Israel. And there shall not be an old man in your house forever.'" (1 Sam. 2:27–32)

The older generation cannot condemn the next generation for their behavior if they have not taught them. Some of you have heard me say how consistently and regularly I would sit down and talk with my children about the heritage God had given us through my forefathers. Heritage had a direct impact on my family.

God did not call out four from my dad's side of the family to be Baptist pastors, training at Spurgeon's college, only to shut it all down in my generation. When I came along, I could never forget what God did in my heritage. So I told our children all the mighty moments that God had performed in my life, so they would be sensitive to God in their lives.

I would tell them how I met Marilynn, their mother. They needed to know how I met Marilynn. They had no idea of what I said to her and how she responded to me when God put us together. I shared the wonderful way in which God made her a summer missionary in Canada before we met. I shared how the wonderful plan and purposes of God unfolded in the families we came from. I shared with them my sense of call into the ministry. I can remember talking to them and saying that when I was a little boy, probably around nine years of age, I had an encounter with God during which He convinced me that He was God and I was not!

From that day to the present my life has been radically changed. When I enter the presence of God I say, "Oh God, You are God and I am not. I am not here to instruct You or counsel You or tell You what I want You to do. I am here to acknowledge that You are God and I am not. Now speak to me, Lord. Show me Your ways."

Did my children need to know and understand the process that God has taken me through? How did their dad get to do what he is doing today?

They needed to know that it was purely the choice of God. Is it any wonder that our four boys and one girl wanted to serve the God they saw and knew their dad and mom served?

What happens if you fail to tell the next generation of God's activity in your life? What happens if you feel your only responsibility is to make sure they attend Bible study at church? Or what comes to pass if your child makes a profession of faith and is baptized merely with the hope that he will at least attend church when he gets older, and there is no sense of heritage or call before God?

Thus, how did there come four hundred years of dark days for God's people just before Samuel's time? There arose a generation of people who knew neither the God of their fathers nor the mighty deeds God had done. The people of that day achieved their own goals but put their generation in bondage over and over again.

GOD'S ANSWER TO BONDAGE

Then God came. He stepped in and brought onto the scene a man named Samuel. The definitive word in the book of Judges is, "In those days there was no king in Israel; everyone did what was right in his own eyes" (17:6).

Do you understand how critically dangerous it is to go your own way without any reference to what God has been doing? Any generation of God's people who have a pattern in their lives to do what is right in their own eyes have lost the truth that they are a corporate and covenant people of God.

We are a part of the royal priesthood. The priesthood of the believers is never in the singular but always in the plural. No priest functions outside the corporate priesthood of the believers. In our generation many believe they can do what is right in their own eyes, without reference to anyone else.

Even the Lord's Prayer starts, "Our Father." Listen to many people pray, and you will notice they do not have a corporate dimension in their prayers.

They are not thinking of their brothers; they are thinking of self and what they want to accomplish. They tend to think of their gifts, their ministries, and their abilities. Many tend to go off and do "their ministry" regardless of what anyone else thinks or says. That is totally contrary to the ways of God.

Doing what is "right in [your] own eyes" is what put the people of God in four hundred years of bondage. Then comes Samuel, and you have a brand-new story. God assigned this moment to Samuel.

"Then I will raise up for Myself a faithful priest who shall do according to what is in My heart and in My mind. I will build him a sure house, and he shall walk before My anointed forever" (1 Sam. 2:35). This verse carries with it so much that is in the mind and heart of God. (Later on, in Chapter 8, we'll see how although raising his sons should have been a defining activity for Samuel, he did fail in this crucial issue.) When I lay this verse over my own life I feel so unworthy. I do not know how to deal with it. I say, "Lord, would You do something in me to rearrange my life to meet Your will? Help me to see this from Your perspective. Help me to understand that the generation that preceded Samuel included Eli the priest. He did his own thing, and had forgotten the mighty deeds of God. He never taught his children." Chapter 4 of 1 Samuel deals exclusively with the judgment of God on Eli and his sons. Chapter 2 also deals with judgment on Eli. In the middle of this story, you hear the heart of God.

I want you to see this from two perspectives:

1. You need to see the heart of God. What has God always been looking for? Then, what does God look for when He comes to your life? What is He looking for in our generation? Does any of this match your life—not because you say it does, but because God has confirmed it Himself?

2. You need to see the heart of Samuel as he responds in his relationship to God.

Jesus had a way of helping people see the condition of their hearts. He said, "These people draw near to Me with their mouth, and honor Me with their lips, but their heart is far from Me" (Matt. 15:8). Nowhere in the Bible is it recorded that out of your head come the issues of life. But the Bible does declare, "Keep your heart with all diligence, for out of it spring the issues of life" (Prov. 4:23). If you want to know if you are responding to God with your head or your heart, look to see what is coming out of your life. You cannot have a good tree and bad fruit (Matt. 7:18). Whatever is in your heart will come out in your life. Our tendency is for each of us to do our own thing and blame everybody else for the conditions of our ministries. I refuse to do that. I lay the Word of God over my life and ask the Holy Spirit to help me understand what God is saying. Then I ask God to radically deal with me to see if everything in my life lines up with His heart. In other words, is my life being lived at the center of His will? You will find this process throughout the Bible. But quoted here it is so incredibly clear: "Then I will raise up for Myself a faithful priest who shall do according to what is in My heart and in My mind. I will build him a sure house, and he shall walk before My anointed forever" (1 Sam. 2:35).

God raises up servants for Himself! There is essentially no other force at work. It is Him! He does not provide servants for the time in which we live, or for the lost, or for missions, or for any other person or purpose. When God raises up someone, He always raises that one up for Himself. He does not do this merely for an activity in one's life.

RELATIONSHIP OR RELIGION?

God has delivered a message through my life dealing with the fact that we, as the people of God, have moved from a relationship to a religion. We are doing pretty well in our activities, but the nation is going to hell. While our churches grow and our buildings are built, lives are not being transformed, and God's eternal purposes are not being fulfilled in us as I believe God intended. We are accomplishing religious activities and all the while missing out on an abiding relationship with Christ.

Notice that this desire for a relationship is consistent with the heart of God. In Exodus 19, God entered the first covenant with His people. He said, "You have seen what I did to the Egyptians and how I bore you on eagle's wings and brought you to Myself?" (v. 4). Relationship was what God was helping the people to remember.

God's original call was to Himself, not to a place, a position, or an assignment. If you neglect developing your personal relationship with God, you have tainted the essence of why He called you. You must have a significant time with God—not thirty minutes of devotional time. I am talking of a life that is anchored in a relationship with God twenty-four hours a day. A servant has no time off. A servant relates to his master twenty-four hours a day. If you are to serve Him as you should, you must know Him, hear Him, and obey Him. You cannot say you know Him merely with your head. For example, all the seminary training in the world cannot be a substitute for a relationship with God. You can have your head full of all the knowledge the seminaries can provide, read the books they assign, and still not have a relationship with the living God.

It is not more head knowledge we need; it is a heart relationship we must develop. Why? First, because He calls you to Himself. Second, God revealed His heart in this call of Samuel when He said, "I will raise up for Myself a faithful priest."

Not long ago when a part of God's people were in great turmoil, I was aware of seventeen pastors who resigned their churches on one weekend. I talked with one of them. He was a significant leader among God's people, and this is what I heard him say: "There was great conflict in my church, and I did not want to be perceived as being a part of that, so I resigned."

When I heard that pastor's response, God brought to my mind the passage in John 10. Jesus said, "I am the good shepherd. The good shepherd gives His life for the sheep" (v. 11). Jesus went on to describe the enemy of the flock: "But a hireling, he who is not the shepherd, one who does not own the sheep, sees the wolf coming and leaves the sheep and flees; and the wolf catches the sheep and scatters them. The hireling flees because he is a hireling and does not care about the sheep" (John 10:12–13). Our problem is that we do not immerse ourselves in the Word of God. When the enemy comes in the midst of the flock, the shepherd should lay down his life for the sheep. The shepherd will not abandon the sheep. *Involvement* is the key word as it relates to a shepherd and his sheep. Sheep are always under his care and keeping—unless he has lost the shepherd's heart!

God has to have somebody in the midst of His people because there are "false prophets, who come to you in sheep's clothing, but inwardly they are ravenous wolves" (Matt. 7:15). They come "to steal, and to kill, and to destroy" (John 10:10). We have wolves all over the world. They look like sheep. But do you know how you can tell if they are sheep? If they create friction, division, death, and destruction, then they are neither sheep nor shepherds. Calling them "sheep" does not mean that they are sheep. If the by-products of their lives are stealing and destruction and killing, then they are wolves in sheep's clothing. Identify them. Stand against them. But if the shepherd leaves the sheep, the sheep do not know the difference. Often when the shepherd has fled, the flock is devastated. Some churches may never recover enough to be what they used to be. Today, God is still looking for faithful priests.

FAITHFUL PRIESTS

What is God looking for? When He was looking for Samuel He said, "I will raise up for Myself a faithful priest." We need to redefine "raise up for Myself." Not in terms of our culture, not in terms of our friends, but in terms of the heart of God. God's purpose in working through a faithful priest is to effect His purposes in His people. God said He was looking for a "faithful priest."

How, then, did God define a "faithful priest"?

First and foremost, a faithful priest is one "who shall do according to what is in My heart and in My mind" (1 Sam. 2:35). Oh my! Do we not need to return here again and again so that we can say beyond a shadow of a doubt, "The heartbeat of everything I am and everything I do is what is on the heart and mind of God"? It is not what is in your heart, nor what you want to accomplish for God, nor what you want to see in your church, nor even what you want to see in your group of churches. The key is not what you want to see (your vision), but what is in God's heart and what is in His mind.

Many of you have as a promise for yourself, "For I know the thoughts that I think toward you, says the LORD, thoughts of peace and not of evil, to give you a future and a hope" (Jer. 29:11). Do you know what is in the heart of God and in the mind of God? God was going to raise up Samuel. Out of all the people in the Old Testament, I have come to love Samuel, for he was a man who knew the heart and mind of God. He faithfully shared it in a most difficult time when the people chose not to follow. He stayed with them all the way through. He remained a faithful priest to God and to His people.

Did God accomplish His purposes? God raised up the first of His prophets and preserved His people even while disciplining His people. God had a man whom He raised up to become a faithful priest who knew and followed and did what was in the mind and heart of God—for His people.

Characteristic of Samuel, the man God raised up for Himself, was his integrity before God! He was God's servant. He knew this and never forgot it all the days of his life. Whenever God had a crucial word for His people, He told Samuel and Samuel faithfully shared it with God's people. Often it was a word they did not want to hear—but Samuel shared it anyway. This was true with his very first assignment as a mere boy. He told Eli that God was going to take Eli's life and the lives of his sons because of their sin (see

1 Sam. 3). This awful assignment from God was part of the call. God knew His people needed to know and hear what was in His mind and heart. He had to have someone who would be impeccably faithful to Him in delivering to His people what was in His mind and heart. So He raised up such a man—Samuel!

Would you let God raise up such a person in our day if you knew that person would be you? And if you know He has indeed done this in you, are you clearly faithful to know and share in our day what is in the mind and heart of God?

We have the example in Samuel. Now it is our turn!

You and I are the beneficiaries centuries later. God left us a spiritual legacy in the life of Samuel. We are the beneficiaries of a man called Samuel—raised up by God for such a time of crisis in the midst of His people.

Finally, God promised Samuel a "sure house." With Samuel, I do not believe it was his sons, but rather a "school of prophets" who carried on Samuel's prophetic role in the midst of God's people. In the Scripture, there is no clear connection between Samuel and a subsequent prophet. Perhaps Nathan, who later confronted David about his sin, had been trained by Samuel, who confronted King Saul with his sin. God always had a timely prophet who would speak clearly a word from God to the kings of Israel and Judah in a time of spiritual crisis. It seems to have begun with Samuel and continued throughout biblical history.

God has always raised up a faithful priest for Himself in every generation. He is not about to leave our generation without His clear voice through His chosen servants.

SAMUEL MINISTERED TO THE LORD

Then Elkanah went to his house at Ramah.
But the child ministered to the LORD before Eli the priest.

1 Samuel 2:11

FIRST SAMUEL 3:1 BEGINS, "Now the boy Samuel ministered to the LORD." I hope that you will take that verse seriously and meditate on that phrase for both your life and your ministry. You do not primarily minister to people; you minister to the LORD. In Ezekiel 44:10 the Scripture says, "And the Levites who went far from Me, when Israel went astray . . ." God consigned the Levites to minister in the temple. They would open the doors and regulate the people, but they would not stand before Him. Then God said, "But the priests, the Levites, the sons of Zadok, who kept charge of My sanctuary when the children of Israel went astray from Me, they shall come near Me to minister to Me" (Ezek. 44:15). Is there a difference between being called to minister before God and ministering before the people? You are of no use to God unless you understand what it means to minister to God. He called you where? To Himself! To be for Him a faithful priest unto Him.

> **You are of no use to God unless you understand what it means to minister to God.**

17

Destruction will come to the people of God if there is not a faithful priest who will minister to God. Another Scripture says, "So I [the Lord] sought for a man among them who would make a wall, and stand in the gap before Me on behalf of the land, that I should not destroy it; but I found no one" (Ezek. 22:30). How significant is it to be called as a servant to serve before God? The one who serves before God will hear things from God that other people do not hear. He will be like a spiritual watchman on the walls of the people of God, as in that striking passage in Isaiah 62:6–7: "I have set watchmen on your walls, O Jerusalem; they shall never hold their peace day or night. You who make mention of the LORD, do not keep silent, and give Him no rest till He establishes and till He makes Jerusalem a praise in the earth." This amazing word becomes an immediate standard for your life and ministry.

The little boy Samuel "ministered to the LORD" (1 Sam. 3:1), and "grew before the LORD" (1 Sam. 2:21). Our tendency may be to say, "Oh, he just had the job of lighting the candles." But that is not so. That unique phrase, "grew before the LORD," is found all the way through the Bible. It reveals a very special assignment from God. In 1 Samuel 2:35 the Scripture says, "I will raise up for Myself a faithful priest."

That phrase can help us to take a personal spiritual inventory. This Scripture describes what God is looking for in a servant of God. You can either be a faithful priest to the people or a faithful priest to God. Now God says, "I will raise up for Myself a faithful priest who shall do according to what is in My heart and in My mind." That means if you are going to be a servant of God you need to be what Samuel was. He ministered to the Lord. And you are going to see very quickly that when Samuel ministered to the Lord, he was in the presence of God and God spoke to him.

Ministry to the people will give you opportunity to hear what the people want and what the people say. But if you minister to the Lord you will hear what the Lord says and what the Lord wants. Please make sure you know the difference. Can you minister to the people and to the Lord?

Absolutely! Service to God does not mean you do not minister to people. But the primary focus is that God called you to Himself to minister to Him. God knows that there are some things He wants to say to His people. God also knows the people will never have a chance to hear from Him unless you get your messages from Him. You will see this as you study God's activity in the life of Samuel. But remember this, Samuel's ministry, as God saw it, was very similar to Ezekiel's. The Scripture states, "As for them, whether they hear or whether they refuse—for they are a rebellious house—yet they will know that a prophet has been among them" (Ezek. 2:5); and, "when this comes to pass—surely it will come—then they will know that a prophet has been among them" (Ezek. 33:33). Whether or not the people would ever hear Samuel, they would know a prophet had been among them.

Look at the context of Samuel's ministry. First Samuel 2:12 tells us that "the sons of Eli were corrupt; they did not know the LORD." Verses 13 and 14 describe the priests' blatant disregard for the holiness of the Lord's offering:

> And the priests' custom with the people was that when any man offered a sacrifice, the priest's servant would come with a three-pronged fleshhook in his hand while the meat was boiling. Then he would thrust it into the pan, or kettle, or caldron, or pot; and the priest would take for himself all that the fleshhook brought up. So they did in Shiloh to all the Israelites who came there.

Verses 22 through 25 describe their evil dealings with the people:

> Now Eli was very old; and he heard everything his sons did to all Israel, and how they lay with the women who assembled at the door of the tabernacle of meeting. So he said to them, "Why do you do such things? For I hear of your evil dealings from all the people. No, my sons! For it is not a good report that I hear. You make the LORD's people transgress. If one

man sins against another, God will judge him. But if a man sins against the LORD, who will intercede for him?" Nevertheless they did not heed the voice of their father, because the LORD desired to kill them.

Why was this so? "The word of the LORD was rare in those days; there was no widespread revelation" (1 Sam. 3:1). This was the context of Samuel's ministry! Most of his ministry was not one in which the people would hear and obey the Word of God as delivered by Samuel. Consequently, they were in constant trouble. But in the midst of this godlessness, the Scripture tells us again and again that Samuel ministered before the Lord: "Then Elkanah went to his house at Ramah. But the child ministered to the LORD before Eli the priest" (1 Sam. 2:11); and again, "But Samuel ministered before the LORD, even as a child, wearing a linen ephod" (1 Sam. 2:18). Last, the Scripture states, "Now the boy Samuel ministered to the LORD before Eli" (1 Sam. 3:1).

VISION OR REVELATION?

What about your ministry as a parent, a pastor, or a person in the business world? Are you going to minister to the Lord? Carefully observe the context in the first verse of 1 Samuel 3: "And the word of the LORD was rare in those days; there was no widespread [or open] revelation." Many in our day do not operate by revelation but by vision. Because many have so adapted to the world, they have let the world's method of leadership control them. The world's thinking says that you cannot be a leader unless you have vision. However, the people of God are not to be a people of *vision;* they are to be a people of *revelation.* Is there a difference? There is! Do you know why the world has to have *vision* for what they want to accomplish? The world does not know how to hear God through His Word. They do not know or even choose to know God, or what He would reveal. So they must have their "own vision." I have been in hundreds of conferences where the leader has asked, "What is your vision of what you want to accomplish over the next five years?" That is the wrong question. We are not a people of *vision*—we are a people of *revelation*. We are a covenant people. We belong to God. We have no business telling God what we want to accomplish for Him or dreaming up what we want to do for God.

Proverbs 29:18 has been interpreted by many as, "Where there is no vision, the people perish (KJV)." A descriptive translation describes the verse like this; "Where there is no revelation, the people cast off restraint (NKJV)." My translation is, "When they do not have a word from God, everyone does what is right in his own eyes." When believers are not hearing from God, there will be spiritual anarchy in the lives of the people of God. They do what their own minds want to do. Rebellion and chaos will allow people to do what their own hearts design to do and to defy anybody to deny them that right.

> **We are not a people of *vision*—we are a people of *revelation*.**

Spiritual anarchy in the lives of the people of God will bring great distress. There was no open revelation of God in Samuel's beginnings. Even the word of the Lord was scarce. If the word of the Lord is rare, the messages, or sermons, from the spiritual leaders will be quite different from what they should be. There is a profound difference between a *sermon* and a *word from God*. Crafting a *sermon* from your own mind and heart is possible, but you have to get a *word from God* out of a relationship with Him. Be very cautious—do not tell the people you have a *word from God* unless you have sat in His presence and received a word from Him for His people. Listen to the Lord of hosts:

> Do not listen to the words of the prophets who prophesy to you. They make you worthless; they speak a vision of their own heart, not from the mouth of the LORD . . . For who has stood in the counsel of the LORD, and has perceived and heard His word? . . . But if they had stood in My counsel, and

had caused My people to hear My words, then they would have turned them from their evil way and from the evil of their doings. (Jer. 23:16, 18, 22)

Do not sit down and craft a sermon from your mind and the notes of others and say you had a word from God. He must guide you in all sermon preparation or Bible study, and it is critical for you to know that you have a word from God.

Once you have a word from God you need to ask Him to help you put it together in such a way that a child could understand that truth from God. Two things I constantly pray before I speak publicly are, "Lord, what is it that You want these people to hear at this time? Help me to understand the particular truth that could set Your people free." And second, "Once I sense the truth that You desire, then would You enable me to say it in such a way that a ten-year-old can understand it and know what to do with it?"

A WORD FROM GOD

Profound differences between Samuel and the priests and the Levites (including Eli) are seen in 1 Samuel. God raised up Samuel and plunged him into the midst of the covenant people of God. They had the law, all the commandments, and all the guidance of God. It was all there. But the "word of the LORD was rare." Were the priests doing their job? Was Eli doing his job? Why was there no open revelation of God? Because the people had long since departed from an intimate relationship with God. This was going to be a constant pattern in the rest of Scripture. Samuel was like a spiritual watershed or turning point. God was going to do things to shape his life that would become a pattern for all the prophets to come. The contrast between a person who has a word from God and a person who dreams up what he wants to say, even if it comes from Scripture, will be constant and profound.

Jesus turned to the Pharisees in John 5 and made this statement: "You search the Scriptures, for in them you think you have eternal life; and these are they which testify of Me. But you are not willing to come to Me that you may have life" (vv. 39–40). Think about the people of God in our day. Many have forgotten that the Scriptures bear witness to Christ. The Scriptures do not give you life; they simply reveal where the Life is. They reveal the Person whose nature is life. But is it possible to study the Scriptures, even preach from the Scriptures, without an abiding relationship with Christ? Is it possible to preach week after week and month after month, yet somehow not lead God's people to make the connection that the Scriptures are not an end in themselves, but a means to an end? It is possible. Jesus explained this in John 5 as He spoke to the leaders and the teachers of the Law. They would not let the Scriptures bring them to Him. So I ask you the same questions that I ask myself. Are you speaking out of the technicalities of the Scriptures? Or have you gone through those Scriptures to the relationship and now bear witness to the relationship? Then are you seeking to lead the people of God through the Scriptures into the vital and exciting relationship with God Himself as revealed in Scripture?

A TURNING POINT

In the very first verse of 1 Samuel 3, the setting for God's initiative in Samuel's life is incredible. The word of the Lord was very rare. Also, the Scripture says that "in those days; there was no widespread revelation." The revelation of God should have been the way in which God's people functioned. Instead there was no open revelation. It was not happening. Though all the religious leaders were in place, doing their duties, the people were not receiving a word from God.

Change began to take place when God dealt with Samuel. The whole situation was different when God began to work. Not only was the situation different for Samuel, the situation was completely different for the entire people of God. When the servant of God speaks a word from God, the people of God can return to God and find fullness of life in Him. I have always thought that when God is about to do a mighty work He causes a child to be born. From and through that child comes the fulfillment of His mighty purposes. I felt the significance of that when I held our firstborn son. When God is about to do a mighty work of revival and awakening in the land, He causes a child to be born. God may have put that child in your home. So have you looked at each of your children, saying, "Is this child one that God has chosen for such a time as this? How then should I watch over this one whom He has given us?"

When God shapes a servant, it will always affect an entire people of God. You need to understand that. For example, you do not sin in private. God has created you in such a way that any sin in your life is going to dramatically affect all the people of God. When you sin—that will affect the rest of the body. If you have cancer, sooner or later it will affect your entire body. And that is supremely true of a leader. The degree to which you let God shape and mold you is the degree to which He will shape the entire people of God.

When Samuel began ministering to the Lord, there was no open revelation. At the conclusion of 1 Samuel 3 (v. 21), God "revealed Himself to Samuel in Shiloh by the word of the LORD." God was now revealing Himself again. Revelation was now present in the people of God.

RETURNING AGAIN!

Observe this twenty-first verse to see what God did at this moment in Samuel's life. "Then [after He had shaped and guided and confirmed and affirmed the one He had chosen] the LORD appeared again." That word *again* is very important in this context. "Again" is the definition of revival. God returns to His people as He used to—again!

Do you remember a time when the Lord was powerfully present in your life, or the life of your church? Can you remember when people just approached the place of worship and came under conviction? Have you ever experienced those moments? Not everyone has had those experiences. God has graciously allowed me to experience some of those moments. I remember moments when complete strangers walked through the entrance to the church and there was a trembling in their hearts that they could not understand.

While pastoring in Saskatchewan we met many people from different religious backgrounds. Many had never been in a protestant or evangelical church. Many of them later told me they could not explain what happened when they walked through the door of the church. They said that they "felt the awesome presence of God." Do you remember a time in your church or in your ministry when that was the case? If not, you may now be looking at your ministry or church saying, "Will You not revive us again, that Your people may rejoice in You?" (Ps. 85:6). In other words, what exists today is not what used to be.

Was there a time in the history of God's people when the presence of God was incredibly real? Yes! God's presence was real when they entered the covenant relationship with God in the first place (Ex. 19–20). Remember how God did it? He did it through thunder, lightning, earthquakes, smoke, and fire. Exodus 20:20 records that the people were scared out of their wits. Moses had to comfort them, saying, "Do not fear; for God has come to test you, and that His fear may be before you, so that you may not sin." God came near to them to see what was in their hearts, and to create a sensitivity to sin.

The conscious, experiential presence of God is the greatest single deterrent to sin. But not just the presence of God so that we say, "He is here!" and use the proof text that "where two or more are gathered, there am I in your midst" (from Matt. 18:20). That verse is wonderful and very true. But there is a difference between head knowledge and an encounter with God.

25

When God encounters His people, He does it in a way that the fear of God grips the heart and mind and soul. Sin is exposed immediately. People cry out to God, "Oh God, forgive me!"

The accounts of the great awakenings and the great revivals tell the story.

> In January 1907 God was moving in a powerful way in North Korea, and a Western missionary recalled one particular scene: "As the prayer continued, a spirit of heaviness and sorrow for sin came down upon the audience. Over on one side, someone began to weep, and in a moment the whole audience was weeping. Man after man would rise, confess his sins, break down and weep, and then throw himself to the floor and beat the floor with his fists in perfect agony of conviction. My own cook tried to make a confession, broke down in the midst of it, and cried to me across the room: 'Pastor, tell me, is there any hope for me, can I be forgiven?' and then he threw himself to the floor and wept and wept."[1]

In the presence of God there is an awesome fear of God that He knows us and knows our sin and knows what we are doing with it, and we fear Him. Have you been there?

I had the privilege of being the campus speaker at Howard Payne University just a few years ago. God had already been mightily at work at Coggin Avenue Baptist Church in the community. Before I arrived there they sent me a few articles from the campus paper. The stories shared that there was a fear that had come over the campus. The students began to gather to pray. Students could be found praying under trees, in the doorways, and in the classrooms. Students prayed early in the morning and sometimes all through the night. The whole campus was in prayer. They knew that God was there and that God was about to do something very extraordinary.

On the second night of our meetings, the Spirit of God suddenly moved upon the gathering. Two outstanding students, who were leaders on the campus, simply ran to the front of the room and came up on the platform.

As they came running up they said, "We've been trying to repent privately and God won't let us repent in private! We've got to do it in public."

I responded to them saying, "Then let me guide you as you repent. Come to the microphone."

The first young man said, "You know me as one who is a leader of Bible studies. I preach because I have been called to ministry, but my heart is full of pornography and sin. God has convicted me of that, and He won't let me confess privately. I have to confess it publicly and acknowledge it to you. And to you girls, I have sinned against you because I have looked at you and lusted after you." He cried and he wept. When he had finished I said, "Sir, you need to go to the back of the platform, kneel to pray, and cry out for mercy."

Mercy was what they needed as they came into the awesome presence of a Holy God. Many books have been written about grace, but preceding grace is mercy. God's nature, revealed to Moses, was—My *name is mercy.* This is described in Exodus 34:6–7 in this way: "And the LORD passed before him and proclaimed, 'The LORD, the LORD God, merciful and gracious, longsuffering, and abounding in goodness and truth, keeping mercy for thousands, forgiving iniquity and transgression and sin, by no means clearing the guilty, visiting the iniquity of the fathers upon the children and the children's children to the third and the fourth generation." Before God can give you what you do not deserve, He will have to withhold from you what you really deserve. God must first cancel your sin. When you cry out to God for mercy and plead with Him to extend His mercy to you, you do so because you have sinned grievously against a Holy God.

As that young student prayed, you could hear his cries going to God. Then the other young man came, who had a similar testimony. What do you do when God is present? You let Him complete His work! So I simply said to the group, "It is obvious that God Himself is among us. I just somehow sense that among the rest of you men there may be many who now are in the presence of the almighty God and have come under grave conviction of your sin."

During this chapel time, students came to the platform and fell to their knees crying out to God. Other students began to share as I guided carefully. Then a young female student said, "You fellows think you are the only ones who have sinned. God has convicted me that I have sinned. I and others have sinned against you young men by the way we have dressed. We have dressed inappropriately and caused you to sin. God has told us we need to confess that and ask you young men to forgive us, and I have asked God to forgive me."

I asked her to go over by the piano and pray to God, telling Him what she had just expressed to the group. As she fell on her face and began to sob, the place was filled with the sounds of the coming of the Spirit of God. I invited others to come if God Himself had exposed this sin to them. Many others came and literally fell over the chairs to get to the place of meeting with Almighty God.

Some of those students were so moved of God that they traveled to Southwestern Seminary in Fort Worth, Texas, during the next few days and gave testimony in their chapel service. So deep was the movement of God at Southwestern (two of my children were in the service when those students gave their testimony) that they shut down all the classes. Two young men who were ready to graduate announced they had never been saved. God had convicted them of their sin.

Some students went up to Wheaton College, and for a whole week the Spirit of God fell on that campus. Several hundred other campuses were touched with the Spirit of God.

Then the Lord appeared "again." Maybe there are some of you who have never yet been in a moment when God tabernacled among His people. Maybe your heart is still longing for Him, because the "word of God is rare" in your life and experience.

THE END PRODUCT

Look at the end product of what God did after He had shaped and molded a young man called Samuel. What Samuel experienced is what happens when God has His servants in place. Yet we must not simply observe what happened in Samuel's life, but what happens when God has your life in place. What will happen in your church or your community when God has you in the place where He can entrust you with an encounter? The problem with the people in Samuel's day was that they had become so disoriented to God, there was no open revelation.

Things change drastically when God reveals Himself. The Scripture says, "For the LORD revealed Himself to Samuel in Shiloh by the word of the LORD" (1 Sam. 3:21). Why? Because Samuel was one who now knew God and would know it was God when He revealed Himself. When the relationship with God is in place, you will know how serious a situation is with God and what you need to do next.

Revival is to me, in its basic definition, God present and real again in the midst of His people. But when we have no reference point to that, we say, "Well, God's with us every Sunday." The issue is not just to know He is with you on Sunday, but if you can tell someone about the encounter you just had with God! What happened when God met with you last Sunday? It is an awesome thing to know what really happened when God made Himself present. To tell the people that He is with us in all of His power when there is no evidence of it in our lives is a betrayal of God's people. The absence of God's presence is what led the people of God into four hundred years of bondage. There was no open word from God. But in Samuel's day, God came again; He appeared again, "in Shiloh."

God has specific places of meeting. Any old place is not always acceptable to God. While pastoring a church early in my ministry, God began approximately thirty-eight mission churches and none of them were the same. We started churches in all kinds of places. But you'd better be careful that you have freedom from God to meet where you choose to meet. In the Old Testament God mandated that His people meet *where* and *how* He said to meet. It is critically important to understand that God had established a place of meeting for the people of God. It was a place called Shiloh. If God was going to show up again it would be a place of appointed meeting. And that was in Shiloh.

"For the LORD revealed Himself to Samuel in Shiloh" (1 Sam. 3:21). Now connect these two phrases: "The LORD appeared again," and "the LORD revealed Himself to Samuel . . . by the word of the LORD." There is an astounding connectedness between those thoughts. Read them again and put your life alongside it, as I put mine alongside it.

"*Then* [after the prerequisites were in place] *the LORD appeared again . . . For the LORD revealed Himself to Samuel . . . by the word of the LORD.*" That is revival. All the people knew that Samuel was an approved servant of God when God revealed Himself to Samuel. You will not receive a hearing nor do you acquire a reputation of being a servant of God because you announce it, or simply because you call for an affirmation of your ordination. Self-appointed affirmation does not make you a *spiritual leader* nor does it make you acceptable to the people. You have to earn the reputation.

In 1 Samuel 4, when crisis fell upon the people and the ark of the covenant was captured by the Philistines, guess what they did? The people came to Samuel and beseeched him to intercede for them before God. Why did they come to Samuel? Why didn't they go to Eli? They went to Samuel because God had confirmed that Samuel was His servant (1 Sam. 3:20).

Let me ask you: Do people seek you out for intercession on their behalf, not because you are the pastor, but because the word is out that God is your guide? When people have come to you, have you gone into the presence of a Holy God for direction? If you did, you entered into the most holy place by the blood of Christ through a new and living way, His broken body, and you have gone "behind the veil"—and when you go there (see Heb. 10:19–20) all heaven responds. That is why people will seek you out! You have a spiritual reputation!

As a pastor, I took spiritual inventory constantly and regularly. I would ask myself the question, "Are the people of God seeking me out in their times of utter tragedy? Am I called on having been shaped as a servant of God for times of crisis?" In times of crisis, does anyone turn to you? Or does no one think of turning to you? Oh, but you fill a position. That may be about all you do. The test of whether you are of use to God is whether the people of God, in time of crisis, seek you out. They do not come to you because you are the pastor, but because you are a servant of God. And they know that when you go into the presence of God He hears you and will reverse some things, or bless because of you. Does your own family turn to you in their time of need?

In times of crisis, does anyone turn to you?

So here is the end product. The front end of this passage begins by saying, "Now the boy Samuel ministered to the LORD before Eli. And the word of the LORD was rare in those days; there was no widespread revelation." And then it ends with, "Then the LORD appeared again in Shiloh." Revival among God's people!

After four hundred years there was now a new beginning. God had found someone He could trust. God had found someone who was wholly God-centered.

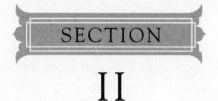

SECTION

II

HONORED BY GOD

"For this child I prayed, and the LORD has granted me my petition which I asked of Him. Therefore I also have lent him to the LORD; as long as he lives he shall be lent to the LORD."

1 SAMUEL 1:27–28

THREE

A GODLY FATHER AND MOTHER

Then they rose early in the morning and worshiped before the LORD,
and returned and came to their house at Ramah.
And Elkanah knew Hannah his wife,
and the LORD remembered her.

1 Samuel 1:19

ONE CANNOT EXAGGERATE THE IMPORTANCE of godly parents. This is true in the mind and heart of God, as seen in the Scriptures, and in the life of those God uses mightily, like Samuel. God certainly can, and does, use anybody. But He seems greatly desirous of giving godly parents to those He would use greatly among His people. Parents seem to be carefully selected to give birth to, and raise before the Lord, those God is purposing to use. This was true of Moses, Samuel, and later John the Baptist and Jesus. The parents are known to God as faithful and godly before Him. Seeing their faith, He chooses them to have a child He plans to use for His eternal purposes.

I see this in my own life. I have also noticed this in the life of those He is greatly using among His people in our day. And this truth has greatly motivated me to be a godly parent and raise my children to please God, so that He could, if He chose to, use each of our children in His purposes. All four boys have felt called to be pastors and are serving the Lord faithfully.

Our daughter is a career missionary in Europe. All of our children are also aware of the influence of their lives on our thirteen grandchildren.

It is important to note that God many times mentioned the parents of the ones He used mightily in the Scriptures. However, it certainly does not mean that God did not use others whose parents were not mentioned. For example, He used Mary Magdalene, Matthew, and others in a mighty way, yet there is little, if any, information on their parents.

Godly parents are vital. They create the spiritual atmosphere in which a chosen servant of God will be raised and nurtured and remain faithful throughout his life. The parents' godly lifestyle will be one of the greatest influences shaping any servant of God. I think of Timothy. God intentionally mentions his mother and grandmother as a crucial gift of God to his life (2 Tim. 1:5). He was the product of his godly heritage.

Godly parents are vital.

Samuel's father is mentioned in 1 Samuel 1:1–2, "Now there was a certain man of Ramathaim Zophim, of the mountains of Ephraim, and his name *was* Elkanah the son of Jeroham, the son of Elihu, the son of Tohu, the son of Zuph, an Ephraimite. And he had two wives: the name of one was Hannah, and the name of the other Peninnah. Peninnah had children, but Hannah had no children." The Scripture then states, "This man went up from his city yearly to worship and sacrifice to the LORD of hosts in Shiloh" (1 Sam. 1:3). This yearly worship, traveling to Shiloh as God had requested, reveals a faithful heart and example before his family.

Worship, affirmed and led by the father in the home, is vital. Throughout every mention of Elkanah, Samuel's father, he is leading his family not merely in worship, but in *faithful* adherence to all the commands of God in the Law. Every mention of his name links him with faithfulness to God, kindness, and tenderness to his wife Hannah. He is a leader in his home, and his example affected Samuel, leaving similar character qualities in his young life, and later his walk with God.

HANNAH AND ELKANAH'S RELATIONSHIP

He would give "portions" to each of his wives, but it clearly states, "to Hannah he would give a double portion, for he loved Hannah, although the LORD had closed her womb" (1 Sam. 1:5). Elkanah was very mindful of Hannah and expressed his great love for her constantly. She needed this assurance and love, for she had no children and was ridiculed constantly by Peninnah (1 Sam. 1:6–7). This became a refining and testing time for the future mother of one of the greatest judges and prophets in all of Scripture.

How she would handle rejection and ridicule, and even great sorrow and pain, would create an atmosphere in her home that would have a solid character-shaping effect on Samuel, enabling him in his lifetime to have these same qualities in his relationship with God. Hannah turned to the Lord in prayer for help. It is so obvious that she not only believed in God, but knew His faithfulness and trusted Him completely. She somehow knew that God would hear her cry, when she cried unto Him day and night. Jesus demonstrated this same confidence in His heavenly Father as He instructed His disciples that "men always ought to pray and not lose heart" (Luke 18:1). Jesus spoke a parable and then applied it, saying, "And shall God not avenge His own elect who cry out day and night to Him, though He bears long with them? I tell you that He will avenge them speedily" (Luke 18:7–8). Hannah knew God this way, and prayed. God heard her, and Samuel was born.

Little did she know how her calling on God and trusting Him would affect Samuel. Little did her husband know of all Samuel would mean in the eternal economy of God's purposes for His people. As Elkanah watched his wife Hannah, he encouraged and supported her walk before God.

How crucial it was for him to support Hannah. She lived before him in a way that convinced him of her sincerity and godly character. He believed in her. How much they shared together about her burden the Bible does not say. But Samuel's father did what every father must do. He gave utmost support and encouragement in every aspect of his wife's burden. And he led the way to the house of God to worship, and it was there that she prayed so earnestly.

Clear obedience is established as a value in the home, but an essential in all of life.

The bonding between husband and wife (and later father and mother of Samuel) was crucial for the establishing of the character of God's chosen vessel. It seems that in all of Hannah's time of distress and uncertainty the key remained: "They rose early in the morning and worshiped before the LORD" (1 Sam. 1:19). So many godly characteristics develop in worship. Many of these are caught by the children. Certainly, the place and quality of prayer are vital. Confident expectation of God's faithfulness to His people is secured. Clear obedience is established as a value in the home, but an essential in all of life. These were learned in regular worship, led by the father and shared by both parents.

THE PRAYER LIFE OF HANNAH

The significance of Samuel's mother, Hannah, cannot be conveyed in words; nor can words express or properly evaluate her importance. This is especially true of her prayer life, which later became so crucial in Samuel's life. So many of God's finest have had godly mothers who were great prayers! This is still true! The prayer life of the parents dramatically affects the life of the children. This is true in my own life as well. I had godly parents who prayed faithfully and observably before each of our family. This has been true of my wife's parents too. The effect has been significant. My wife and I have also sought to be faithful, intense pray-ers for our children. Our children have responded also to God's claim and call on each of their lives. Each of them is also a pray-er. They in turn are teaching *their* children to pray.

A careful look at the prayer life of Hannah reveals several important details:

1. "And she was in bitterness of soul, and prayed to the LORD and wept in anguish" (1 Sam. 1:10). Her prayer life was intense and would not be denied, for she believed God could and would hear her prayer for a child. The effect of a mother's prayer life is profound! History is full of accounts of this phenomena. Oh, that more mothers in our day would seek to emulate Hannah in prayer. How many godly young men and women would be available to God and His purposes? Her prayer habits were clear and relentless. God deliberately gives a glimpse into her actual prayer and praise in 1 Samuel 2:1–10. We will look into this later. This was more than likely a mere sample of her praying. As Samuel grew he heard her pray often with great praise and thanksgiving, knowing that he was born in answer to his mother's praying, and his father's support. What a heritage! We need to ask crucial questions concerning our lives also, such as: "What is the open character and quality of our praying before our marriage partners, and our children?" And, "Do husbands and wives pray together so that the particular burden God may lay on one can be shared and carried by the other?"

2. She was focused. She knew what her request was, and she was not casual or distracted. Focused prayer! Specific prayer! Earnest prayer! Here is a key to Hannah's prayer life: She knew what was on her heart; she knew therefore what to pray and was relentless and would not stop praying until God answered her. What about our praying? Are we specific, or are we always general and nonspecific? Many simply pray, "God bless everyone." God desires specific praying, for He gives specific answers. A church must be this way also, especially in public worship, before the hearing of all God's people.

3. "Then she made a vow" (1 Sam. 1:11). What a serious moment before God! A vow! Heard by God and kept by Hannah. To God, a vow is a solemn promise—to Him! Ecclesiastes 5:2, 4–5 indicates the heart of God toward a vow:

> Do not be rash with your mouth,
> And let not your heart utter anything hastily before God.

For God is in heaven, and you on earth;

Therefore let your words be few . . .

When you make a vow to God, do not delay to pay it;

For He has no pleasure in fools.

Pay what you have vowed—

Better not to vow than to vow and not pay.

God knew her heart! And God set in motion how He would respond through Eli, who was watching her pray.

4. Her prayer was between her and God alone. She had not told Eli of her broken heart before God. He observed her and misunderstood her heart condition before God. Eli was evidently not a man of prayer as he ought to have been, but this did not deter Hannah. Too often we let the unspiritual lives of our leaders affect our prayer lives and therefore deny ourselves the incredible answers God would bring to us. Hannah was alone in her prayer burden. God saw it and gave her full assurance through Eli. When Eli knew her plight in prayer, he blessed her and said, "Go in peace, and the God of Israel grant your petition which you have asked of Him" (1 Sam. 1:17).

5. Hannah believed God in her heart and everything was now changed, "So the woman went her way and ate, and her face was no longer sad" (1 Sam. 1:18). She believed that she had received God's answer and she was about to obtain it. In the New Testament, Jesus said:

Have faith in God. For assuredly, I say to you, whoever says to this mountain, "Be removed and be cast into the sea," and does not doubt in his heart, but believes that those things he says will be done, he will have whatever he says. Therefore I say to you, whatever things you ask when you pray, believe that you receive them, and you will have them. (Mark 11:22–24)

Oh, the simplicity of believing prayer. How our lives and our nation/world should and could be changed by the praying of His people!

Just as God had promised through Hannah's "pastor," Eli, she was given a child! Such a significant pattern of God is now revealed: "The LORD remembered her" (1 Sam. 1:19). Here is the centerpiece of prayer—the sovereign faithfulness of God to His Word. Right on schedule, that is, God's purposed schedule, "Hannah conceived and bore a son, and called his name Samuel, saying, 'Because I have asked for him from the LORD'" (1 Sam. 1:20). Oh, the significance of a name! Hannah's son's name—Samuel—literally means "heard by God."

This "heard by God" would characterize the entire life of Samuel. Is it not a point of wisdom to watch and respond to the love of God in the birth of each of our children, and name them accordingly—especially according to the faithfulness of God in our lives and home? Do not merely pick a name out of a book, unless the name matches your response to the activity of God in your life and family. Can you imagine Samuel's name being a witness before everyone as he was growing up—"heard by God"? They would be saying as he passed by, "There goes 'Heard by God.'"

HANNAH'S VOW TO GOD

As time went by, Hannah never forgot her vow to God, and neither had God! She returned to Eli in the temple, and before God and Eli she said, "For this child I prayed, and the LORD has granted me my petition which I asked of Him. Therefore I also have lent him to the LORD; as long as he lives he shall be lent to the LORD" (1 Sam. 1:27–28).

Several wonderful character-building qualities are found in this response to God's provision through her praying. First, she kept her vow to the Lord, even when it meant separation from her son. Since God gave her Samuel, he belonged to God, and Hannah would not fail to release him back to the Lord. We did this with each of our children. Later, when God called each of them to serve Him completely, we once again gave them back to the Lord in full and joyful release.

One of the greatest stumbling blocks to many who are called by God into missions is the parents. They resist this call, for they know that not only their children, but their grandchildren will not be close by. What a tragedy for any Christian to withhold from the Lord a child whom God has given him or her! Many receive a child from their Lord and never acknowledge that the child belongs to the Lord, and should be at His disposal and at His call. Hannah was not this way with Samuel, and the world came to experience the greatness of her child as he served the Lord. "So they worshiped the LORD there" (1 Sam. 1:28).

Here we can only speculate about the heart of Eli as all this took place. He was not walking with the Lord, nor was he teaching and instructing his sons, Hophni and Phinehas. This failure would ultimately become the deaths of Eli and his two sons (see 1 Sam. 2:12–17, 22–34). But as Hannah and Elkanah worshiped with their son, Samuel, God must have pricked Eli's conscience, giving him one more warning about his sons. But Eli did not listen, for he had become unfamiliar with God's voice. Eli now had no intimacy with God. This came at a crucial time in the life of God's people, when he needed to know what was on the heart and mind of God. God had to raise up someone else who would hear Him. How tragic! He could not play "catch-up" when God needed him most. So he did not recognize the true nature of Hannah's heart. When she first prayed, Eli accused her of being drunk. Now Hannah had to remind him of that moment and her sacred vow to God. Eli, too, had made vows to God about raising his sons before the Lord. He had failed, and it would be unbelievably costly to both him and his sons.

I remember praying early in our marriage: "(1) Lord, help us to live in our relationship with You daily in such a way that all of our children would want to choose to serve the God they see us serving; (2) help me to recognize clearly when You are dealing with each of my children, and help me to be available to You and to them to help them understand and respond to Your encounter." God granted both of these requests. But I had to be sincere, focused, and watchful. I could not be distracted or careless in my walk with God and His activity in our children around us.

THE PRAYER OF HANNAH

Now comes one of the most profound moments in all of recorded Scripture—the prayer of Hannah, recorded in 1 Samuel 2. This is a masterpiece in prayer, to be studied by all who would be raised to a new level of prayer before God. Here are some of the highlights that can be studied carefully for your own life, church, or ministry. There seem to be two parts to her prayer:

1. thanksgiving and praise;

2. prophecy about the sovereignty of God over His enemies (God's people were now slaves to the Philistines [1 Sam. 4:9]).

Hannah, the mother of Samuel, gave God only her best. Nothing less was acceptable to God. She wanted to be the kind of mother that could receive a son from the Lord and give him back to God with character qualities God would use for Himself. So she had to be the kind of mother who would model character qualities for her son. We need to look at her prayer as a means of revealing her heart and character toward God.

First, here are the things Hannah says about God, whom she served:

Her "heart [rejoiced] in the LORD" (1 Sam. 2:1). The joy of the Lord was her strength. She was a happy person in her relationship with God. She set the atmosphere in the home, and her husband rejoiced with her. She created an atmosphere of joy in the Lord. Whatever the Lord brought her way, she accepted with gladness. She anticipated the goodness of her Lord and rejoiced. This was a deep-seated character quality in her life, and it was passed on to Samuel.

My home was this way also. Joy filled our home. But not just any joy. It was joy in the Lord. Our family went through many deep waters, but the joy of the Lord carried us through. Because this was true in our home, my life has always been full of the joy of the Lord. In the home God let me establish, joy has been a lifestyle for us and our children. We notice that every time we are in our children's homes, they are full of laughter and joy in the Lord. It is always a delight for us to visit our children and their children. Joy is always sooner or later the focus of our conversation.

Her "horn [strength]" was "exalted in the LORD" (1 Sam. 2:1). Every mother and every home needs the strength of the Lord. But it must be a character trait in the parent before it can be experienced in the home. Hannah obviously drew her strength from her Lord. She knew Him. She cried out confidently to Him. She received her strength from Him. Everyone around her saw this and were themselves strengthened. She had many occasions to need God's strength, but none was more obvious than when, year after year, she was unable to have a child. This was a burden and a grief to her. Her need for daily strength from the Lord was obvious. God granted her request. Here, in her sacred prayer, she acknowledged where her strength came from, and how it seemed to increase and sustain her. It was from her Lord. Reading of the life of Samuel, it is so very clear that daily, in the midst of the sin of the people of God and the ruin caused by their enemies because of their sin, Samuel needed an ever-enlarging source of strength. Because he saw and experienced the strength of the Lord resting on his mother, he then knew where he would turn when he needed strength for his life.

The strength that comes from a confident faith in God was always so evident in our home. Once when I was a child, our family was at our summer camp about four hundred miles from home. My dad lifted a heavy boat, and tore a valve in his heart. The doctor that examined him warned Dad that he could not be moved, but Dad insisted on going home.

My dad gathered our family (three sons and my mother) around his bed, told us what the doctor had said (the doctor gave Dad a letter absolving him of all medical responsibility if my father did not obey him), and added, "God has assured me that we are to travel home, and He will take care of us. Mother, you drive, prop me up in the backseat, and let's begin our trip" (a four-hundred-mile trip over dirt roads and many mountains). We made it home safely. Dad walked up two flights of stairs and was immobile in bed for the next three months with a torn valve in his heart. He trusted what God said to him. In our eyes and hearts Dad had a great track record of listening to and obeying his Lord. This character trait was passed on to me. I have never doubted God since that day, and I have lived by faith in a faithful God, who protects us as we live before our five children. They, too, have this character trait in their lives to this day. Hannah's faith in her Lord, expressed in her prayer, set a tone to develop a solid character of faith in Samuel.

She rejoiced "in [God's] salvation" (1 Sam. 2:1). Hebrews 2:3 speaks of "so great a salvation." Hannah was aware of the greatness of God's salvation, and she lived in it, rejoiced in it, and bore witness to it. She knew clearly what it meant to be a vital member of a covenant people of God. All the promises of God to His people *were hers* and she lived by them. She knew He would withhold nothing good from those who walked uprightly.

> For a day in Your courts is better than a thousand.
> I would rather be a doorkeeper in the house of my God
> Than dwell in the tents of wickedness.
> For the LORD God is a sun and shield;
> The LORD will give grace and glory;
> No good thing will He withhold
> From those who walk uprightly. (Ps. 84:10–11)

45

How could anyone live faithfully before God, and His people—a life of knowing and trusting in God's great salvation—and that life not influence others? Samuel discovered the greatness of God's salvation as he lived in a godly home. This great salvation and faith were lived out and proclaimed by his mother, Hannah.

What is the understanding of God's great salvation that your family gets from your life? Is it faithfulness to God? Is the power of the Cross seen in and through your life? The power of the Resurrection, or Pentecost? Is it revealed in the way you live? All these, and more, are a vital part of God's great salvation. Not only that, but the people of God themselves are an essential aspect of God's great salvation, provided for everyone who participates.

"No one is holy like the LORD" (1 Sam. 2:2). A sense of the holiness of God filled Hannah's heart and life, and she expressed it so freely here. She would not violate anything God had commanded, and her husband joined with her in all she did. She fulfilled the Law, as she knew it, and God honored her for it. Samuel was born in a home permeated with a sense of the holiness of God. Sin was therefore abhorrent to her, and thus to Samuel. The holiness of God in Samuel's life left him with a healthy *fear* of God. Though all Israel lost the fear of God, Samuel never did. I believe it was because of the lives of his mother and father. A healthy attitude against sin in a home is an expression of the character of holiness in the life of the parents. What we watch and read, how we make decisions, the values we establish—all reflect our experience with the holiness of God. Hannah affected Samuel by her understanding and response to the holiness of God.

"There is none besides You" (1 Sam. 2:2). Hannah knew God. She knew He was the only God. Therefore she shunned all other pretenders of God. She lived in the midst of the gods of the surrounding nations, but she never gave in to them. She worshiped God only! She openly acknowledged this before everyone, which was unusual in her day, as the people were worship-

ing "the other gods" that surrounded them. This was a major reason God kept judging them. But Hannah remained absolutely true to God alone! For Samuel, this became an established conviction in his own life and character. No wonder God chose to hear Hannah's prayer for a son. He knew she would be a clear example before her son of the God she served. How very important this is in our own day. Our children *must* see God, and Him only, in all we do. They must see us resisting the world's attempts to conform us to its thinking and living (see Rom. 12:1–2).

"Nor is there any rock like our God" (1 Sam. 2:2). God was her stability. Her God was not like shifting sand—unstable for building. When God is the Rock for a believer, it means he or she is confident about God in both the present and the future. God would not be moved by anything or anybody. They could count on Him at all times, in all conditions. It is like the counsel Paul gave to the Corinthians: "And God is able to make all grace abound toward you, that you, always having all sufficiency in all things, may have an abundance for every good work" (2 Cor. 9:8). To believe Him in this way is to develop a character quality of dependability and steadfastness. Hannah lived this, and so Samuel was immersed in God as his Rock. This conviction was needed throughout the life of Samuel. He gained it from his mother and father at home.

"The LORD is the God of knowledge" (1 Sam. 2:3). To Hannah, the wisdom of God and the knowledge of God were totally sufficient for her life. She acknowledged this to God in her prayer, and to the people around her. As she prayed with such confidence in God, Samuel would hear and develop his own trust in the knowledge of God that he would use in his tumultuous life. God never failed to tell Samuel what to do and what to say to His people. As a result, the people responded to him, and he responded to God. Samuel never let his understanding come before God's knowledge in any situation. He developed as a man who knew what was in the mind and heart of God—and did it. This is what God was looking for. Samuel learned so much from his mother and father.

"By Him actions are weighed" (1 Sam. 2:3). For Hannah, God knew everything she did and measured it against what He had commanded in the Law. God weighs every action of His people against His guidelines of what He has commanded. If a person was living faithfully by all He commanded, He weighed his or her life and found it acceptable and pleasing and He blessed that person. If He weighed the people in their actions and found them wanting (less than He commanded), He judged them and did not bless them. Hannah knew this and lived in the "fear of the LORD" as God had commanded. She feared lest she not be pleasing to God in all she did, and God blessed her. This became a character quality in the life of Samuel too. And God blessed him also.

What about your life? Do you thoroughly realize that God is weighing every action in your life? Do you know He is responding to you according to what He finds? He gives to us according to our works (see Ps. 62:12; Matt. 16:27; Rom. 2:6; 1 Cor. 3:8).

What a prayer! What a personal expression of confidence in God. What a model for each of us in our moments of crisis. While she prayed, her husband, Elkanah, was present, listening and worshiping with her. Verse 11 indicates that when Hannah had finished praying, "then Elkanah went to his house at Ramah." He had entered into the vow of his wife, for verse 11 then says, "But the child ministered to the LORD before Eli the priest."

It is interesting to see how God worked in the lives of others in a similar way. Their walks with God were revealed when they prayed, also, and their lives also deeply affected their sons. Certainly Elizabeth and Zacharias, and their son, John the Baptist, are evidence of this similar relationship with God. The prayer of Zacharias is also very classic. It is found in Luke 1:68–79. This is also true of Mary, the mother of Jesus. Her extraordinary prayer is found in Luke 1:46–55. Their predictions concerning the enemies of God's people are similar to Hannah's. Mary's song in Luke 1:51–54, was a response to the prophesy stated in Luke 1:45:

Blessed is she who believed, for there will be a fulfillment of those things which were told her from the LORD.

Zacharias's prophecy follows in Luke 1:71, 74.

There is also a prophetic word Hannah included in her public prayer about how God would defeat all the enemies of His people. No one would withstand Him (see 1 Sam. 2:4–10). Little did she know (maybe she did, the Scripture does not indicate) that it would be her son, Samuel, whom God would use to bring about such a victory for His people. In every revelation of Himself to His servants, God makes known not only His blessing on His faithful people, but His judgment on those who do evil against His people. This is seen all through Scripture. A simple passage is Psalm 1:

Blessed is the man
Who walks not in the counsel of the ungodly,
Nor stands in the path of sinners,
Nor sits in the seat of the scornful;
But his delight is in the law of the LORD,
And in His law he meditates day and night.
He shall be like a tree
Planted by the rivers of water,
That brings forth its fruit in its season,
Whose leaf also shall not wither;
And whatever he does shall prosper.
The ungodly are not so,
But are like the chaff which the wind drives away.
Therefore the ungodly shall not stand in the judgment,
Nor sinners in the congregation of the righteous.
For the LORD knows the way of the righteous,
But the way of the ungodly shall perish.

> **How very important it is that we give close attention to the activity of God in our lives.**

How very important it is that we give close attention to the activity of God in our lives. We, too, must learn to pray and sing, even in public, concerning the faithfulness and goodness of God to His people. We must also give courage to His people about the victory God will bring to them. When He does bring great revival among His people He will also bring an awakening in the nation. This potential for revival can begin with the influence of a godly father and mother.

FOUR

HONOR

And the word of Samuel came to all Israel.

1 Samuel 4:1

"THEN A MAN OF GOD CAME TO ELI and said to him, 'Thus says the LORD: . . . "For those who honor Me I will honor, and those who despise Me shall be lightly esteemed"'" (1 Sam. 2:27, 30). Here is the setting for an amazing revelation of the heart of God and the ways of God among His people. Nowhere in the Bible is this truth stated so clearly. And nowhere is it implemented so immediately and dramatically as in the lives of Samuel, Eli and his sons, and the people of God.

God, by His very nature, is gracious toward His people. He is also full of mercy. Again and again He sends messengers to His people to warn them when they are straying far from Him and are continuing in that attitude of heart and life. God's people had continued for four hundred years to stray from God and their covenant with Him. In His fullness of time, He sent a man not only to warn His people and His faithless leader, Eli, but He was also at this moment pro-nouncing a significant transition. Eli and his sons would die, and God said He would "raise up for Myself a faithful priest who shall do according to what is in My heart and in My mind" (1 Sam. 2:35).

> **God, by His very nature, is gracious toward His people.**

51

God, in love, would seek to lead His faithless covenant people back to their covenant relationship with Himself.

Through this unknown "man of God," God stated once more His covenant with His people. He had made this covenant years earlier through Moses, who said to them:

> Now it shall come to pass, if you diligently obey the voice of the LORD your God, to observe carefully all His commandments which I command you today, that the LORD your God will set you high above all nations of the earth . . . But it shall come to pass, if you do not obey the voice of the LORD your God, to observe carefully all His commandments and His statutes which I command you today, that all these curses will come upon you and overtake you. (Deut. 28:1, 15)

The entire twenty-eighth chapter of Deuteronomy spells out in great detail this covenant.

This man of God was now delivering the message from God to Eli and the people of God that *those who honor God, God will honor, and those who do not honor God, He will lightly esteem.* This message would now ring down through the rest of time for God's people, and God would say this in a thousand ways and times, both warning and encouraging His people to walk faithfully with Him in His covenant with them. This is His invitation to His people of every generation to this very day. He comes to each of us, to our churches, and to every larger convocation of His people. God continues to say to us, "I love you. I chose you, and have been working in you to make you an instrument of My grace to a lost world. I *am* the Potter. You are the clay. Yield to Me fully, and you will be greatly used by Me in your world!"

From Adam and Eve in Genesis to John and the churches in the book of Revelation, God clearly tells His people of His measureless love for them. He gives the conditions for experiencing His love uninterrupted by sin or rebellion. With Adam and Eve, He said if they obeyed Him and His words

52

to them, He would bless them without measure. To Abraham, when He called him, God promised not only to bless him and his descendants, but through him "all the families of the earth shall be blessed" (Gen. 12:3; Acts 3:25). He assured His people before Him at Mount Sinai, "You shall be a special treasure to Me above all people" (Ex. 19:5). This promised covenant was stated throughout the Old Testament. It appeared again as Jesus invited His people to experience in their lives the fullness of the kingdom of God. He said that "it has been given to you to know the mysteries of the kingdom of heaven, but to them [others] it has not been given" (Matt. 13:11). To help His disciples realize how open-ended the blessings of God were to them, He added: "Whoever has, to him more will be given, and he will have abundance" (Matt 13:12).

GOD'S COVENANT—
THE NEW TESTAMENT PERSPECTIVE

The reality of the covenant relationship in God's kingdom is still valid, extensive, and crucial for God's people to understand in every generation. The apostle Paul, throughout his life and to the very end of his life, was constantly found "preaching the kingdom of God and teaching the things which concern the Lord Jesus Christ with all confidence, no one forbidding him" (Acts 28:31).

The apostle Paul had an extensive and deep understanding of God, and an experiential relationship with Him. He was also thoroughly acquainted with the Old Testament Scriptures, especially God's covenant with His people. Paul knew what God was doing. He also knew God's presence and power. So he did all he could to teach and preach to God's people that they were heirs to Abraham, and through them all the nations of the earth would be blessed.

So diligent was Paul's faithfulness to God, that God's people believed God, and were used of God to turn the world upside down (see Acts 17:6).

God has worked all through history with such power in and through every generation of His people who believed and obeyed Him. But it is also true that in each generation God raises up for Himself someone through whom He can challenge His people to such a saving relationship with Himself.

In Samuel's day God sent "a man of God" to once again remind His people of the faithfulness of their covenant-keeping God. He had promised, and now would once again honor those who honored Him. Here, and in every generation, God's people had to decide:

1. Did they believe God?

2. Would they remain faithful to the covenant God made with them?

3. Would they bring their lives into the covenant relationship that they had entered with God?

4. Would they then listen to God, hear His voice, and obey Him?

5. Did they now expect God to do mighty works through them, as He had done with their fathers?

When God's people realized they had departed from God and then returned to Him, God brought revival. Revival is simply God returning to His people in all His fullness and power, and demonstrating His presence in His people to a watching world.

This is our greatest need today. But most of God's people do not believe they have moved away from Him. Their religious activity continues, causing them to believe they have not departed from Him. But too often when the covenant (i.e., the clear commands of Christ) are placed alongside their lives, their families, or their churches, it is very clear that they are now living a long way from the expectations of God. Consequently, they are content to live without the manifest presence of God. Because of this absence of the mighty power of God in and through His people, the world has little or no encounter with God.

As clearly and intentionally as God sent a man of God to Israel in Samuel's day, so He sends messengers to us. In the New Testament Jesus often said to God's people, "He who has ears to hear, let him hear!" (Matt. 11:15; 13:9; Mark 7:16; Luke 8:8; 14:35; Rev. 2:7, 11, 17, 29). I pray that not one of us, especially the spiritual leaders, fails to hear and obey Him. However, Jesus said to those in His day that His people killed the prophets God sent to them (see Matt. 23:31, 37; Acts 7:51–53).

John, in exile on the Isle of Patmos, was also hearing from God about His activity in His world through His covenant people. God was now working in the churches Christ had established throughout the world:

> The Revelation of Jesus Christ, which God gave Him to show His servants—things which must shortly take place. And He sent and signified it by His angel to His servant John, who bore witness to the word of God, and to the testimony of Jesus Christ, to all things that he saw. Blessed is he who reads and those who hear the words of this prophecy, and keep those things which are written in it; for the time is near. (Rev. 1:1–3)

THE COVENANT RELATIONSHIP

Overwhelmingly basic in its promise, God's statement in 1 Samuel 2:30 is so significant for God's people. I have given an entire chapter to unfold carefully the implications found in God's promise to "honor those who honor [Him]." This promise is another way of expressing His original covenant with His people.

This covenant was expressed first in Exodus 19 and 20. Its essence is in what we call the Ten Commandments. The covenant is spelled out more extensively in passages such as Deuteronomy 28 and Leviticus 26. Read these carefully in your Bible, or you may turn to Appendix A, where you will find them in their full text.

This covenant says: *If* you will . . . then I will; *If* you do not do . . . then I will not do. The blessings promised are extensive and only things God could do. The *curses* for disobedience are God-like, and God-sized too. Both the *blessings* and the *curses* reveal to a world the nature of God, especially His holiness! To read and understand both of these passages is to tremble before Holy God just in knowing the nature and conditions of this covenant relationship. God Himself emphasized repeatedly, "Do you not fear Me? . . . Will you not tremble at My presence . . . ?" (Jer. 5:22). Whenever the people of God lost their sense of the *fear* of God and no longer trembled in His presence, their hearts departed from Him and they began to sin and rebel against Him.

It is of no minor significance that when God first gave His people the privilege of entering such a covenant relationship with Him, He deliberately gave it in such a way as to create *fear* in them:

> Now all the people witnessed the thunderings, the lightning flashes, the sound of the trumpet, and the mountain smoking; and when the people saw it, they trembled and stood afar off. Then they said to Moses, "You speak with us, and we will hear; but let not God speak with us, lest we die." And Moses said to the people, "Do not fear; for God has come to test you, and that His fear may be before you, so that you may not sin." So the people stood afar off, but Moses drew near the thick darkness where God was. (Ex. 20:18–21)

This factor—the loss of the fear of Holy God—is nearly always at the root of all sin, even in our own day. When God's people lose their *fear* of God, they soon lose their *fear* of sin. When they lose their *fear* of sin, they depart from God and become of little use to God. Then God sets about, in mercy, to discipline them so they will return to their covenant with Him. Once

Israel agreed to this covenant, God held them accountable to their promise. Theirs now was to be a life of *faith*. This has always been God's way. But faith, from God's perspective, is never based on what you do not know, but what you do know. It rests on what you believe about *Him*. Once you

When God's people lose their *fear* of God, they soon lose their *fear* of sin.

believe Him, then obeying Him and what He commands is the only possible response that is worthy of Him. To disobey Him, in the mind of God, is to depart from Him. No one can stay in a healthy and vital relationship with Him and not obey Him.

To help us know how God sees this matter of "departing," you must hear clearly from Him. In Deuteronomy 30:17, God declared: "If your [1] heart turns away [departs] [2] so that you do not hear, and [3] are drawn away, and [4] worship other gods and [5] serve them . . ."

It begins when the "heart turns away." He told them: "You shall love the LORD your God with all your heart, with all your soul, and with all your strength" (Deut. 6:5). When their love for God turned away, their whole lives turned away, and the covenant with God was broken.

When their hearts turned away, they would no longer hear or obey His voice. When they were no longer hearing His voice clearly and exclusively, their hearts would be drawn away from Him, and they would then be listening to other voices seeking to take them away from their God. If they followed these other gods, they would then begin to worship them. Ultimately what happens is: What you begin to worship, you begin to serve. This completes the separation from God.

God's people usually try to continue their outward allegiance to God through religious activity. But their ears no longer love and hear and obey the Lord. The prophet Isaiah warned God's people: "These people draw near with their mouths and honor Me with their lips, but have removed their hearts far from Me, and their fear toward Me is taught by the commandment of men" (Isa. 29:13).

Jesus said this was also true of God's people in His day (see Matt. 15:8–9; Mark 7:6–7).

This obedience to the covenant was to be based on an intensity of love—love on God's part, and love on the part of His people. So in the heart of God, if the people ever departed or strayed, it was because they had "left [their] first love" (Rev. 2:4). The only response acceptable then to God was to "remember therefore from where you have fallen; repent and do the first works, or else I will come to you quickly and remove your lampstand from its place—unless you repent" (Rev. 2:5). This continued to be God's simple and clear instructions to individuals, such as David and Peter, as well as to Israel and Judah, and also His people in Jesus' day.

Jesus expressed this relationship between love and obedience clearly:

If you love Me, keep My commandments . . . He who has My commandments and keeps them, it is he who loves Me. And he who loves Me will be loved by My Father, and I will love him and manifest Myself to him . . . If anyone loves Me, he will keep My word; and My Father will love him, and We will come to him and make Our home with him. He who does not love Me does not keep My words; and the word which you hear is not Mine but the Father's who sent Me. (John 14:15, 21, 23–24)

We must realize that when we no longer obey, we have departed from our love relationship with God. To insist that we *do* love God but then never obey Him or even have a desire to know Him or His commands (voice) is to deceive ourselves—but not God!

It is also most instructive for us to realize that when our hearts depart from the Lord, and our lives then also drift away from Him and His will, God does not call for, nor does He accept, what we often call "rededication." The only acceptable response is to follow His command: "Repent, and return to Me!" (see Solomon's prayer in 2 Chron. 6:26–31; 7:12–16). Those who hear Him and repent, He blesses. He honors their response to

His word to them. There is no limit to what He can do, or will do, in the lives of those who repent. Therefore, *repentance* is one of the most *positive* words from God in the Bible!

Repentance brings back the life of God to the sinning child of God. To be cut off from God by our sin is to try to live without the life of God. God expressed this relationship between repentance and the return of the life of God to His people in Ezekiel 18:31–32:

> "Cast away from you all the transgressions which you have committed, and get yourselves a new heart and a new spirit. For why should you die, O house of Israel? For I have no pleasure in the death of one who dies," says the Lord GOD. "Therefore turn and live!"

Repentance is the road to fullness of life from God. This is what Jesus preached: "Repent, for the kingdom of heaven is at hand" (Matt. 4:17).

HONOR HIM, OR BE LIGHTLY ESTEEMED

The phrase "shall be lightly esteemed" (1 Sam 2:30) must be seen also from God's perspective. You must go to the Scriptures to understand its meaning, not to the secular dictionary. Again, the covenant conditions must be read, and read carefully. Any withdrawal or diminishing or withholding of the presence and activity of God is caused by sin and can be fatal. Jesus drew a word picture of this relationship in John 15—the Vine and the branches. Jesus said, "He who abides in Me, and I in him, bears much fruit; for without Me you can do nothing" (John 15:5). Remember what else He said in light of God's promise, "Those who honor Me, I will honor." He who does abide in Christ "bears much fruit" (John 15:5). He went on to say, "By this My Father is glorified, that you bear much fruit; so you will be My disciples" (John 15:8). The Father honors those who honor His Son by abiding in His Son, and He causes them to bear much fruit. However, the other side to this relationship is also seen in this picture: "Every branch in Me that does not bear fruit He takes away" (John 15:2). This "takes away" is as thorough in the New Testament as it was in the Old Testament. It should never be taken lightly, or carelessly. We were, by divine purpose, placed "in His Son" when we were saved, and God's intention has always been that we bear much fruit. If we do, God honors us by pruning us so we can bear more fruit. If we do not, He "takes away" (John 15:2). This is a New Testament way of saying what God was saying to Eli and Israel in 1 Samuel 2:30. This does not mean that we lose our salvation, but we do lose our assignment and no longer bear fruit.

This phrase "lightly esteemed," when it applies to God's relationship to those He has chosen and called and made a covenant with, is very serious. For God to honor a person or a people is incredible. But for God to *lightly esteem* is a fearful statement. It carries with it the withdrawal of the affirming presence of God. It means His blessings are now withheld, including protection, provision, and even victory. Israel would know this in a very costly manner. The enemy (here the Philistines) would defeat them and capture the ark. To Saul, it would mean he would no longer be king, and God's Spirit would be withdrawn. For Eli and his sons it meant they would be killed in battle, and all Eli's descendants would perish.

In our day, to be "lightly esteemed by God" does not carry such ominous implications. But take the definition from God's Word. And what follows this statement in 1 Samuel 2:31–34, 36 *is* God's definition!

The other side of this full covenant relationship with God is clearly seen in the life of Samuel. It is seen first in 1 Samuel 3 as God calls Samuel and then blesses him extensively before all of Israel. God kept His promise in that He honored Samuel in several ways:

- He "called" him, and did it in such a way that Eli would also know it was God. This was important both for Samuel and for Eli. God is complete in all He does (1 Sam. 3:2–10).

- He spoke to Samuel in a prophecy that had far-reaching implications for both Eli and God's people. He predicted Eli's death (1 Sam. 3:11–14).

- It says also, "So Samuel grew, *and the* LORD *was with him* [was honoring him]" (1 Sam. 3:19, emphasis added).

- "The LORD . . . let none of his words fall to the ground" (1 Sam. 3:19).

- Then God made certain that "all Israel from Dan to Beersheba knew that Samuel had been established [confirmed] as a prophet of the LORD" (1 Sam. 3:20).

- Then, most significantly for God's people, as God honored Samuel, "then the LORD appeared again in Shiloh" (1 Sam. 3:21).

- Thus comes the most crucial of all that God does when He honors those who honor Him: "For the LORD revealed Himself to Samuel in Shiloh by the word of the LORD" (1 Sam. 3:21).

    God honors him who honors God by letting him hear His voice. When one—or a church—is not clearly hearing from God, it is because of sin. I have known individuals (especially religious leaders) and churches of whom it could be said, as it was said of the times of Eli and Israel, "The word of the LORD was rare in those days; there was no widespread revelation" (1 Sam. 3:1).

    How many times does God have to declare to us: "If I regard [keep and hold] iniquity in my heart, the Lord will not hear" (Ps. 66:18)?

    For God not to hear means also that the people will not hear a response from God and no further directives from Him for their lives. For four hundred years this was true of God's people until God raised up Samuel for Himself.

- Then it is said, "And the word of Samuel came to all Israel" (1 Sam. 4:1). God now had someone who would honor Him, and

He then, as promised, honored Samuel before all the people. Once again His word came to His people through a faithful priest whom He had raised up for Himself. The one who honors God, He says, always does "according to what is in My heart and in My Mind." God affirms that kind of person completely before His people and a watching world. God honors the one who honors Him. And nothing honors God any more thoroughly than obedience!

FAITHFUL DILIGENCE

Later, when God chose David to shepherd His people (see Ps. 78:70–72), God continued this promise to honor the one who honors Him. This is why David so often cries out confidently to God, "In You, O LORD, I put my trust; let me never be ashamed" (Ps. 31:1). David constantly told God's people, "Let no one who waits on You [in faith] be ashamed" (Ps. 25:3). In other words, he constantly affirmed the faithfulness of God to His covenant people—those who honor Him, He will honor. He will never fail those who trust Him, and therefore honor Him. He will never let their trust in Him end in disappointment. He will remain faithful to His covenant with His people!

Paul put it this way: "All the promises of God in Him are Yes, and in Him Amen, to the glory of God" (2 Cor. 1:20). The apostle many times taught the believers the extensiveness of God's faithfulness to honor those who honor Him with such words as: "And God is able to make all grace abound toward you, that you, always having all sufficiency in all things, may have an abundance for every good work" (2 Cor. 9:8). Those who believe Him and obey Him experience everything God said in these passages. It is His Word (Truth).

An essential character trait in Samuel that guided him always to honor God, and therefore constantly receive the blessings of God, was that he feared God. That is, from the time he was a boy, especially through the nature of God's call in his life, he had a healthy reverence and awe and trembling in God's presence. So later, as he was teaching God's people how to return to God and gain God's forgiveness, he pleaded with them out of his own experience:

> If you fear the LORD and serve Him and obey His voice, and do not rebel against the commandment of the LORD, then both you and the king who reigns over you will continue following the LORD your God. However, if you do not obey the voice of the LORD [do not honor Him], but rebel against the commandment of the LORD, then the hand of the LORD will be against you, as it was against your fathers. (1 Sam. 12:14–15)

Samuel learned that with God, "the fear of the LORD is the beginning of wisdom, and the knowledge of the Holy One is understanding" (Prov. 9:10). God wanted to express His love in His covenant by blessing His people. When they honor Him by loving Him with all their hearts, minds, souls, and strength, and obey all He commands, they therefore greatly honor Him. He in turn honors them. But remember, this is the exclusive life that God promises to the covenant people of God. This promise does not apply to unbelievers. It is found only in the covenant God made with His people, and their faithfulness to Him. However, the world is continually watching God's people. When God's people are honoring their God in obedience, the world comes to know what God is like as He blesses His people. Many in the world then are drawn to Him in a saving way by what they see of God in His people. Often I have seen this happen in a marriage when one is saved. That person's life becomes so different it attracts the other marriage partner to the Lord.

It is important to remember that God's people, during the period of the judges and during Samuel's life, did have this wonderful promise of God— that He would honor those who honored Him. The second giving of the Law (covenant) in Deuteronomy expressed it clearly:

For what great nation is there that has God so near to it, as the LORD our God is to us, for whatever reason we may call upon Him? And what great nation is there that has such statutes and righteous judgments as are in all this law which I set before you this day? Only take heed to yourself, and diligently keep yourself, lest you forget the things your eyes have seen, and lest they depart from your heart all the days of your life. And teach them to your children and your grandchildren, especially concerning the day you stood before the LORD your God in Horeb, when the LORD said to me, "Gather the people to Me, and I will let them hear My words, that they may learn to fear Me all the days they live on the earth, and that they may teach their children." (Deut. 4:7–10)

It may be useful at this moment to review at length a statement of the blessings of God's covenant:

Then it shall come to pass, because you listen to these judgments, and keep and do them, that the LORD your God will keep with you the covenant and the mercy which He swore to your fathers. And He will love you and bless you and multiply you; He will also bless the fruit of your womb and the fruit of your land, your grain and your new wine and your oil, the increase of your cattle and the offspring of your flock, in the land of which He swore to your fathers to give you. You shall be blessed above all peoples; there shall not be a male or female barren among you or among your livestock. And the LORD will take away from you all sickness, and will afflict you with none of the terrible diseases of Egypt which you have known, but will lay them on all those who hate you. Also you shall destroy all the peoples whom the LORD your God delivers over to you; your eye shall have no pity on them; nor shall you serve their gods, for that will be a snare to you. (Deut. 7:12–16)

As the rest of Samuel's life with God unfolds, this incredible promise of God will literally stand out and challenge us in our day to walk faithfully as a

New Testament covenant people of God. Remember, Jesus told His disciples, "This cup is the new covenant in My blood. This do, as often as you drink it, in remembrance of Me" (1 Cor: 11:25). Then, remember how Paul also warned the Corinthian believers of the second part of their covenant by saying:

> Therefore whoever eats this bread or drinks this cup of the Lord in an unworthy manner will be guilty of the body and blood of the Lord. But let a man examine himself, and so let him eat of the bread and drink of the cup. For he who eats and drinks in an unworthy manner eats and drinks judgment to himself, not discerning the Lord's body. For this reason many are weak and sick among you, and many sleep. For if we would judge ourselves, we would not be judged. (1 Cor. 11:27–31)

Here you notice both sides of the covenant relationship with God, now being expressed in the New Testament, and also for us in our day.

Let this promise of God permeate your life completely and personally in your family and in your church, that God may be honored and He may honor you. A watching world will be attracted to God's great salvation through us, His covenant people.

> But now the LORD says: "Far be it from Me; for those who honor Me I will honor, and those who despise Me shall be lightly esteemed." (1 Sam. 2:30)

A man of God was delivering this message to Eli. He was basically saying to Eli, "You have a choice: Those who honor God, God will honor." Is that true in your ministry? Do not take lightly your behavior, lifestyle, and the use of the twenty-four hours you have. You have the same twenty-four hours that I have, or that Billy Graham has. There is not a person who serves the Lord who has more time than you do. Usage of time is the key. How you use the time you have indicates whether or not you honor God.

**Do not take lightly
your behavior,
lifestyle, and the
use of the
twenty-four hours
you have.**

It is not a matter of activity; it is a matter of relationship and resulting obedience to all God in Christ has commanded you.

In reality, the Lord said to Eli, "You have been weighed in the balances and you have been found wanting. You did not honor Me, and therefore are lightly esteemed by Me." Once you know God in His Word, there is not one child of God who would like to hear Him say, "You are lightly esteemed by Me." All of us would want Him to say, "Well done, good and faithful servant. You have honored Me, and I will honor you."

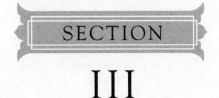

III

CAST OFF BY GOD

Therefore the LORD God of Israel says:
"I said indeed that your house and the house of your father
would walk before Me forever." But now the LORD says:
"Far be it from Me; for those who honor Me I will honor,
and those who despise Me shall be lightly esteemed."

1 SAMUEL 2:30

FIVE

ELI AND HIS SONS

Now the sons of Eli were corrupt; they did not know the LORD.
1 Samuel 2:12

THE SINS OF ELI AND HIS SONS had a profound effect on all the people of God. What they did affected the people during their lifetime and for generations to come. It is never a light matter to be a spiritual leader of God's people and continue in sin, whatever the sin may be. God always sees our lives in detail, and deals with us accordingly. In the corporate covenant with God, it is impossible to sin in secret. Our sin is intimately tied to the lives of all the rest of God's people, especially if we have been called of God to be a leader.

This one family's sin affected the whole nation of Israel, especially the elders and the leaders. The elders lost the ability to make key leadership decisions, resulting in the entire nation's falling into sin and ultimately being put into captivity. Later, David was painfully aware of the effect of his sin on others. So David instructed his son Solomon, who would become king over God's people: "As for you, my son Solomon, know the God of your father, and serve Him with a loyal heart and with a willing mind; for the LORD searches all hearts and understands all the intent of the thoughts. If you seek Him,

> **God always sees our lives in detail, and deals with us accordingly.**

He will be found by you; but if you forsake Him, He will cast you off forever" (1 Chron. 28:9).

This covenant truth was painfully real in Israel, and later when the nation divided, in both Israel and Judah. God knows the heart! He knows when the heart turns away from Him, and He does what He promised in His covenant. He disciplines, judges, and even destroys His people when they turn from Him. The people experience the consequences of sin. It is an awesome privilege to be called of God to be a part of His people with whom He has made a covenant; but it is also an awesome responsibility.

The sin of Eli and his sons also affected Samuel. Samuel did not become a godly *father*, and consequently the sin of his two sons was the motive for Israel's wanting a king instead of God continuing as their King!

Last, the sins of Eli and his sons also affected their own lives. It literally cost them their lives!

One of the great mysteries to me is how godly men can have such sinful and wayward sons, and why God lets it happen. There is little evidence in Scripture that these leaders (Eli and Samuel) faithfully taught their sons the ways of God. Certainly, Eli's life set an example for Samuel, but why did Samuel fail to correct his sons? Did he grow up in a home and a culture where the teaching was left to the mothers? Hannah taught Samuel. Did Samuel then leave the teaching of his sons to his wife and their mother? We do not know for certain. It remains a tragic mystery! But we do know that the covenant required that the parents teach their children diligently all the Law that was firmly in their hearts:

> Hear, O Israel: The LORD our God, the LORD is one! You shall love the LORD your God with all your heart, with all your soul, and with all your strength. And these words which I command you today shall be in your heart. You shall teach them diligently to your children, and shall talk of them when you sit in your house, when you walk by the way, when you lie down, and when you rise up. You shall bind them as a sign on your hand,

and they shall be as frontlets between your eyes. You shall write them on the doorposts of your house and on your gates. (Deut. 6:4–9)

Being a father of five children myself, I have meditated long before these truths. I am as vulnerable as any other person to live carelessly or unfaithfully as Eli did. My children are as capable of leading the people of God astray and away from God as any children because of the nature of my influence on their lives. It is a very serious matter. But the key to a proper understanding of all this is to see it all *from God's perspective*. The Bible is designed to help us walk with God in His blessing and help us avoid costly mistakes, and to follow deliberately in the way of life! Paying close attention to the lives of Eli and his sons, in the midst of God's people, is crucial. I have carefully stood before God on behalf of myself, my children, and the people of God who will be affected by my life. God has been gracious in instructing me and enabling me. Now back to Eli and his sons.

SIN'S PRICE

The Bible is very clear: "Now the sons of Eli were corrupt; they did not know the LORD" (1 Sam. 2:12). Everything that follows—what they did and what God did—is based on this statement.

First of all, it is astounding that the sons of Eli "did not know the LORD"! Can you imagine being the sons of the priest of God yet not knowing God nor the ways of God? They were from the order of priests being set apart by God to guide His people. The sons of Eli offered his offerings and were the people's link with God, His holiness, His ways, and His nature.

In the midst of Eli's failure with his sons, he was confronted by a special man of God. This man reminded Eli of his special heritage. He was especially warned of the seriousness of his actions toward his sons:

Then a man of God came to Eli and said to him, "Thus says the LORD: 'Did I not clearly reveal Myself to the house of your father when they were in Egypt in Pharaoh's house? Did I not choose him out of all the tribes of Israel to be My priest, to offer upon My altar, to burn incense, and to wear an ephod before Me? And did I not give to the house of your father all the offerings of the children of Israel made by fire?'" (1 Sam. 2:27–28)

He then charged Eli with favoring his sons, and honoring his sons, "more than" God (1 Sam. 2:29). In other words, the fact that his sons "did not know the LORD" was due entirely to Eli. He was more concerned about his sons' feelings and responses than he was about his responsibility toward God. He did not teach them the ways of God, especially in the role they were to have in the priestly line. They would follow in Eli's steps, forgetting to guide the people of God in the ways of God. As a result, Eli's sons lived a life of sin—gross sin. They acted as if their lives were without any knowledge of God! The way we live reveals the conditions of our heart toward God.

The Scripture clearly states, "The sons of Eli . . . did not know the LORD" (1 Sam. 2:12). Maybe they were still a part of the remnant of the period of the judges, where it was true that "another generation arose after them who did not know the LORD nor the work which He had done for Israel" (Judg. 2:10). Having been born into the priesthood did not guarantee that they knew God. Having an abiding relationship with God is another matter. They had to be clearly taught and led into this relationship. Having our children baptized, or even that they make a profession of faith, does not mean that they know the Lord. Actually, their lives and conduct will tell if they know the Lord. When I served as a pastor, careless parents said to me, "Pastor, I think that it is time to 'have it done.'" I replied, "What do you mean, *have it done?*" They said, "You, know, Pastor, baptize my child!" To these parents it was not a matter of a vital saving relationship with God in Jesus Christ, but rather a religious practice. This would be fatal! I, of course, sought to teach them, teach them, teach them! Eli evidently did not do this, and his sons did not know the Lord. Their lives then were lived without the Lord. Their life decisions and actions were disastrous not only in their own lives, but in the lives of the people of God as well.

CORRUPTION AND JUDGMENT

Second, as they grew older they were corrupt and lived corrupt lives, dishonoring God by rejecting the commands and statutes of God. Turning aside from all the earnest counsel of the elders who warned them and counseled them, they fell deeper into sin. Then comes a key truth about their sin—it affected God and the people of God: "Therefore the sin of the young men was very great before the LORD, for men abhorred [despised] the offering of the LORD" (1 Sam. 2:17).

How we conduct our worship, as well as other aspects of the Christian life, is not a minor matter. If we worship using the ways of the world, many of God's people will come to "abhor the offering of the LORD." How we lead the Lord's Supper, or Holy Communion, will either endear the people of God to this holy moment or cause many to avoid or stay away from this precious moment in their lives. How we lead in prayer will also attract or deter God's people in their prayer lives. How we lead a time of prayer meeting will either honor God or profane Him, therefore having a severe effect on God's people. Many prayer meetings are awful—even I would not want to attend. The condition of the crucial services of the church is the responsibility of the spiritual leader or leaders.

> **The lives of our children can affect the attitude of God's people toward the Lord and His house.**

So, not only our own lives, but the lives of our children can affect the attitude of God's people toward the Lord and His house. The lives of our children when they were teenagers, and later when they were university students, had a very strong effect on other young people. Fortunately, we gave attention to their lives as they were active in sports and in the youth group. Many unsaved youth were attracted to the church and became Christians. Two of these are now two of our daughters-in-law.

When Eli's sons were corrupt, they acted corruptly. This turned the people away from following God and His ways. When the people, especially the elders and leaders, were not walking in the ways of God, they, too, acted corruptly. They did not know the Lord as God intended, and this affected their judgment in making critical decisions. In fact, their decisions were so far from the ways of God that they caused further captivity and bondage of the people of God and brought further judgment of God upon them.

It was the elders who decided that if they just took the ark of God into battle against the Philistines (see 1 Sam. 4:2–5), it (the ark) would save them from the Philistines. But notice what happened:

> Then the Philistines put themselves in battle array against Israel. And when they joined battle, Israel was defeated by the Philistines, who killed about four thousand men of the army in the field. And when the people had come into the camp, the elders of Israel said, "Why has the LORD defeated us today before the Philistines? Let us bring the ark of the covenant of the LORD from Shiloh to us, that when it comes among us it may save us from the hand of our enemies." So the people sent to Shiloh, that they might bring from there the ark of the covenant of the LORD of hosts, who dwells between the cherubim. And the two sons of Eli, Hophni and Phinehas, were there with the ark of the covenant of God. And when the ark of the covenant of the LORD came into the camp, all Israel shouted so loudly that the earth shook. (1 Sam. 4:2–5)

All the people joyfully followed the counsel of their elders. But this decision was a gross turning from God. Eli should have led them to God for His counsel. But they were so far from God in their hearts that they trusted their own hearts and their own minds.

This judgment of God became the occasion of the deaths of Eli's sons, and ultimately the death of Eli. It also brought about the deaths of thirty thousand foot soldiers. The account of this is found in 1 Samuel 4. Also, the story of the captivity of the ark of God, and the consequent defeat of God's people and the deaths of, first, four thousand men, and then thirty thousand foot soldiers (see 1 Sam. 4:2, 10) is found in this chapter. This judgment of God meant that the people of God did not have the ark in their midst for more than twenty years. During this time, "all the house of Israel lamented after the LORD" (1 Sam. 7:2). It will be important to go back and review again what brought all this trouble.

When Eli was very old we see the pronouncement of God's judgment on Eli and his sons (see 1 Sam. 2:32). Eli tried to confront his sons with their sins and warn them of the consequences: "If one man sins against another, God will judge him. But if a man sins against the LORD, who will intercede for him?" (1 Sam. 2:25). Eli knew that to sin against God was so serious that no one could intercede before God and atone for his sins. But the terrible response of the sons came: "They did not heed the voice of their father." But even more serious is the reason for their response: "because the LORD desired to kill them" (1 Sam. 2:25).

There are several truths about the ways of God here that must be mentioned and studied carefully. God always reads the *heart* and knows the extent and seriousness of the rebellion and hardness. Further, He knows the increasing effect of such a person on the rest of God's people. If God left that kind of person alone, without this person being seriously judged before the watching people of God, then everyone would be encouraged to continue in their own sinful ways. So God closed up their hearts so they could not repent. He would carry out His judgment on them, thus warning the rest of His people. The fear of God would fall on His people and become, at least for the moment, a deterrent to their sin. This He did, and soon "the two

75

sons of Eli, Hophni and Phinehas, died" in battle with the Philistines (1 Sam. 4:11). Not only that, but the consequences remained with Israel for at least twenty years (see 1 Sam. 7:2).

We have a tendency in our day to assume that repentance removes all permanent consequences for our sin. This is not borne out in Scripture or in life. Moses could not enter the promised land because of his sin. A sword remained in David's life all the remaining days of his life. And the consequences of Abraham's sin of unbelief in having Ishmael by Hagar remain with us to this day in the presence and character of the Arab peoples (see Gen. 16:11–12).

Is it possible to be in a position of significant spiritual leadership and lose your family? Both Eli and Samuel lost their families while being the most significant spokesmen for God in their day. In 1 Samuel 2:22 and 1 Samuel 8:1 there is a very sad statement: "Now [and these next few words rang like a bell in me] Eli was very old . . ."; then, "Now it came to pass when Samuel was old that he made his sons [Joel and Abijah] judges over Israel." First Samuel 8:3 states, "But his sons did not walk in his ways; they turned aside after dishonest gain, took bribes, and perverted justice." Then, after examining Samuel's sons, all of Israel, especially the elders, gathered together and demanded a king (see 1 Sam. 8:4–5).

An astounding moment happened at the same time in the hearts of Eli and Samuel, and in the heart of God. There are no moments I know of that equal the moments in which first God announces Eli's and his sons' deaths, and then the moment when Israel asks for a king. Many generations later we see the end product of these two moments in the history of God's people. Israel was completely destroyed, the temple in Jerusalem destroyed, Judah destroyed, and all the people of God destroyed, except the remnant in bondage in Babylon. Seventy years of captivity and misery in Babylon for God's people followed.

If you are ever a God-called servant, remember that what happens with your children will affect all the people of God. Do not take that lightly. You cannot neglect your family while you minister. You cannot say, "Well, I am a God-called servant and I have so much to do." Your family comes first. I have some priorities in my life. God first—and God first does not mean ministry first. God first, my wife is next, and then my children. When Marilynn and I were married, God made us one in flesh and one in spirit. God was a witness when Marilynn and I were married in Trinity Baptist Church in Downey, California. Why did God make us one in flesh and then do something in both of us that was not there before we were married (making us one in spirit)? He did something to change us. He made us one in spirit so that He could never speak to one of us that He was not speaking to both of us. When God speaks to my wife, because we are one in spirit, He has spoken to me (see Mal. 2:13–15).

Why has He done such an incredible work? He is looking for a "godly seed" (Mal. 2:15 KJV). He has something in mind to do through our children. But when we come to this point in the life of Eli, the godly seed was not there, and God's purposes for them were canceled. In Samuel's life the godly seed also was canceled because there was a profound neglect of the family even while he ministered.

> **You cannot neglect your family while you minister.**

The Bible often chooses not to give significant details, which we, of course, would love for God to have made known to us. It was not His choice. However, we do have the consequences of choices made, decisions registered, and words spoken. Here, in both Eli's and Samuel's relationships with their sons, almost nothing is recorded. All we seem to be told is that they chose not to walk in the ways of their fathers. We do know, however, that the lifestyle of the sons deeply affected the people of God—negatively.

So we are left to speculate. But even here we need not depart from the Scriptures. It is enough at this point to remind us that our ministry must not become a substitute or come before the spiritual care of our family. Too many forget that the care of the marriage and the strong spiritual leadership in the family are vital aspects of our total ministry. Our families are to model before God's people all we are teaching them. If God's people are to be praying families, then the leader must openly have a praying family. This is not merely expected by God's people, but by God Himself. This is not too much to ask of a spiritual leader. If you cannot do this, then step down from leadership, for your example of not being a praying family will be too devastating on God's people, and the eternal purposes of God through them may be greatly hindered.

Your ministry to God's people is not a substitute for your ministering before God to your family. God is looking for a godly seed. What you do in your family may determine whether God fulfills a much larger purpose than He ever had with you alone. I expect God, being who He is, to bring much more significance through our five children, all now in ministry, than ever has come from my life. So I keep investing in them. When I am asked to write a book, I turn to the publisher and say, "You asked me to write this book. This is what God has laid on our hearts. But I want to write this with one of my children."

Richard is my oldest son. We have invested in his life. He is the president of the Canadian Southern Baptist Theological Seminary. He is committed to training spiritual leaders who can transform a nation and touch a world. And they are committed to establishing a thousand new congregations in Canada. Richard is at the heart of it to train and equip church planters who are spiritual leaders. Why is it, then, when I wrote the book *Spiritual Leadership* that I asked God to let me write it with my son? I am making an investment in his life. Because God is looking for a godly seed and I am responsible for doing everything I know in the activity of God to work with God in His purposes for each of my children. It has not hindered my service with God; it has enhanced and enlarged my service with God. And I can leave and know that all four boys and our daughter are serving the Lord with all of their hearts. They are serving and writing and are now involved in the kingdom work all over the world.

I say to you, be very careful that you do not put ministry as a substitute for the ministry to your family. The ministry to your family is your ministry—because what you do with your children may ultimately cause the people of God either to walk faithfully with God or to depart. Because of Eli's two sons and Samuel's two sons and their godless behavior, the people abhorred the offerings of the Lord and later pressed God for a king. That set in motion the ultimate demise of the people of God.

THE COST OF DISOBEDIENCE

It is an awesome matter when a father or mother does not instruct their children in the fear of the Lord and does not teach them to walk faithfully in the ways of God. This is even more crucial for spiritual leaders. For the consequences of the leader's disobedience can be very far-reaching and even devastating to the people of God and ultimately to the eternal purposes of God.

First, the sin of Eli and his sons cost them their own lives. God would not relent; He announced that they would all die:

Behold, the days are coming that I will cut off your arm and the arm of your father's house, so that there will not be an old man in your house. And you will see an enemy in My dwelling place, despite all the good which God does for Israel. And there shall not be an old man in your house forever. But any of your men whom I do not cut off from My altar shall consume your eyes and grieve your heart. And all the descendants of your house shall die in the flower of their age. Now this shall be a sign to you that will come upon your two sons, on Hophni and Phinehas: in one day they shall die, both of them. (1 Sam. 2:31–34)

In that day I will perform against Eli all that I have spoken concerning his house, from beginning to end. For I have told him that I will judge his house forever for the iniquity which he knows, because his sons made themselves vile, and he did not restrain them. And therefore I have sworn to the house of Eli that the iniquity of Eli's house shall not be atoned for by sacrifice or offering forever. (1 Sam. 3:12–14)

Samuel was asked to confirm this word from God to Eli, which was given first by the man of God. But the *way* God judged them affected all of Israel. They died in battle with the Philistines, who slaughtered tens of thousands of their finest men, captured the ark of the covenant, and put Israel in distress for twenty years.

Second, the sin of Eli and his sons affected all God's people. The elders became unfamiliar with God and His ways, not having been taught. The elders in turn disoriented God's people, who followed the elders' counsel given out of their own reasoning. Death and destruction became a part of the destinies of both the Philistines and the Israelites (a total of about ninety thousand men died).

Third, their sins seemed to set a pattern for Israel for the rest of their days. Even during His covenant with Israel during Moses' day, God revealed to Moses: "The LORD, the LORD God, merciful and gracious, longsuffering, and abounding in goodness and truth, keeping mercy for thousands, forgiving iniquity and transgression and sin, by no means clearing the guilty, visiting the iniquity of the fathers upon the children and the children's children to the third and the fourth generation" (Ex. 34:6–7).

PATTERNS OF DISOBEDIENCE

Fourth, there is to me an even more significant effect of Eli's disobedience in failing to teach and guide his children in the ways of God—the effect his example had on Samuel. Here we must argue from silence, which is not always safe to do. I believe I am on safe ground, but understand that this is my own observation. It is not insignificant that Samuel followed in the same pattern with his two sons as Eli did with his sons. They did not follow or "walk in his ways [Samuel's ways]; they turned aside after dishonest gain, took bribes, and perverted justice" (1 Sam. 8:1–3). Scripture indicates that "it came to pass when Samuel was old that he made his sons judges over Israel" (1 Sam. 8:1). But, after all these long years as their father, his sons did not follow the Lord as Samuel did. This also caused Israel, led by the elders, to come to Samuel and request a king: "Then all the elders of Israel gathered together and came to Samuel at Ramah, and said to him, 'Look, you are old, and your sons do not walk in your ways. Now make us a king to judge us like all the nations'" (1 Sam. 8:4–5).

We will discuss this crucial moment in the lives of Samuel and God's people in depth later. But for now, it is enough to realize the far-reaching impact of Samuel's failing to teach his sons, as Eli failed to teach his sons. This is a mystery in the Bible. Quite often we see the failure of God's choicest servants to teach their children, and therefore they do not walk before God with integrity. This always had a deep effect on the people of God and consequently on the eternal purposes of God. But the Scriptures do not give any thorough explanation. However, like my own life, this mystery ought not to be lost on the serious follower of Jesus today. The fact remains, though, that some of the children of God's choicest servants do not follow the God of their parents. But there is no doubt about the consequences of parents' failing to teach their children. Every father, especially those called as spiritual leaders of God's people, should seek earnestly the correcting, convicting, and enabling presence of the Holy Spirit to work mightily and consistently in his own life, lest we see this fruit in our lives and homes too!

When Israel asked for a king, and God, seeing their hearts, granted it, it sealed their fate for the rest of time. In seeking a king, they rejected God as their King, and they became like all the other nations. They could not seem to keep their trust in God alone

There is no doubt about the consequences of parents' failing to teach their children.

81

while following a king. No matter how much instruction and warning they received along the way, and how many prophets were sent to warn and instruct them, they seemed to go man's way instead of God's way. The presence of a human leader seems, too often, to bring with it a strong inclination to follow the man, instead of God—unless the man is unusually intimate with God. Significantly, when there is a spiritual leader, there is often a returning to God. Some of the kings sincerely lead the people to follow God and God alone. But the bottom line for the people of God, in Samuel's day, became to follow the king, even when he was corrupt. This put them into bondage and ultimately into experiencing the severe judgment of God, even their destruction.

This pattern, unfortunately, can be seen in individuals, families, churches, and even ministries and denominations. When there are humans who are leaders, not all will be spiritual leaders. When they do not walk faithfully with God and in His ways, the people they lead will follow them to their own destruction. It is at this point that I fall on my face before God and cry out to Him for His enabling grace and mercy and presence to keep me constantly in the center of His will. I must have the continuous convicting work by His Holy Spirit, lest to any degree I should depart from Him or His ways. This is my constant plea before God. The consequences are too incredible, and eternity is at stake in my own life and in the lives of those I lead, including my four boys, my daughter, their families, and the people of God.

GOD MOVES IN THE MIDST OF HIS PEOPLE

One of the most decisive verses in the entire Bible is found in 1 Samuel 2:35. Having pronounced a fatal judgment on Eli and his descendants forever (see 1 Sam. 2:30–34, 36), and reminding Eli and all Israel that "for those who honor Me I will honor, and those who despise Me shall be lightly esteemed" (2:30), God now announces: "I will raise up for Myself a faithful priest who shall do according to what is in My heart and in My mind. I will build him a sure house, and he shall walk before My anointed forever" (2:35).

Here is what God is always looking for: "The LORD has sought for Himself a man after His own heart" (1 Sam. 13:14). God announced that He Himself would have to "raise up for Myself" such a person. This He would do, and that man would be Samuel—which is the reason for this entire book study. Our goal is to know the heart of God and to know the ways of God in the pursuit of His eternal purposes in the world, especially through His own people. We will take our time to study this special activity of God in the midst of His people so that we might be unusually alert to such a move of God in the midst of His people today. It may be in your life, or your home, or in your church! Would you recognize such an activity of God? How would you respond? Would you dare to continue with hardness of heart? Or, would you tremble before God in humble obedience and submission, as Samuel did?

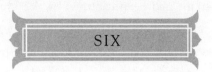

SIX

THE GLORY DEPARTED

Therefore know that the LORD your God, He is God, the faithful
God who keeps covenant and mercy for a thousand generations with
those who love Him and keep His commandments; and He repays
those who hate Him to their face, to destroy them. He will not be
slack with him who hates Him; He will repay him to his face.
Therefore you shall keep the commandment, the statutes, and the
judgments which I command you today, to observe them.

Deuteronomy 7:9–11

ICHABOD, THE NAME ELI'S DAUGHTER-IN-LAW gave to her newborn
son, means "The glory has departed!" (1 Sam. 4:21–22). Having given birth
to her son, she herself died. Tragedy after tragedy!

Ichabod has become a name used in conversation to indicate shame
throughout history. This moment in Israel's history has been remembered to
the present day. From the time I was a boy I can remember my parents and
other adults using this term to describe the final and awful condition of a
person, a city, or even a church. I have heard them say, "It is obvious God
has written 'Ichabod' over that person [or that church]." They meant that
this person or church had sinned so greatly and so long, that it was now
obvious that the presence of God had been withdrawn from them.

God told Eli that he and both of his sons would be killed in battle. Not
only did they die, but Israel's army was also defeated. Even worse than this,

the ark of the covenant had been captured by the Philistines. When Eli heard that the ark had been captured, he fell over backward, broke his neck, and died. Such news about the ark was too much for Eli. He suddenly realized that God had withdrawn His presence from Israel and was no longer protecting them from their enemies.

The covenant clearly stated:

> Now it shall come to pass, if you diligently obey the voice of the LORD your God, to observe carefully all His commandments which I command you today, that the LORD your God will set you high above all nations of the earth. And all these blessings shall come upon you and overtake you, because you obey the voice of the LORD your God . . . The LORD will cause your enemies who rise against you to be defeated before your face; they shall come out against you one way and flee before you seven ways . . . But it shall come to pass, if you do not obey the voice of the LORD your God, to observe carefully all His commandments and His statutes which I command you today, that all these curses will come upon you and overtake you . . . The LORD will cause you to be defeated before your enemies; you shall go out one way against them and flee seven ways before them; and you shall become troublesome to all the kingdoms of the earth. (Deut. 28:1–2, 7, 15, 25)

Phinehas, one of Eli's sons, died in battle; and when his wife heard the news that he had been killed and that Eli had died and that the ark of God was taken, she went into labor and a son was born. Because of this news she named her son Ichabod, saying, "The glory has departed from Israel!" (1 Sam. 4:21). It is stated a second time: "She said, 'The glory has departed from Israel, for the ark of God has been captured'" (1 Sam. 4:22). Then she died!

Eli, the messenger of God for His people, also died on hearing that the ark of God had been captured by their Philistine enemies. This is the record:

"Then it happened, when he [the messenger] made mention of the ark of God, that Eli fell off the seat backward by the side of the gate; and his neck was broken and he died" (1 Sam. 4:18). Thirty thousand men of Israel died in battle that day (see 1 Sam. 4:10), and Israel, the covenant people of God, was defeated.

The sin of God's people is serious with God!

The sin of God's people is serious with God! Sin has lasting effects, especially on all the people of God. When a leader sins, the people tend to follow. There was no greater tragedy than for it to be said of those people that the "glory of God" had departed. For the ark of God to be captured meant clearly that God had not protected it. He had withdrawn His presence, His glory!

Can this happen to the covenant people of God? It did! The record is clear. God hates sin, especially in His people. They know better. Moses had stated this clearly in the very beginning of the covenant:

> For what great nation is there that has God so near to it, as the LORD our God is to us, for whatever reason we may call upon Him? And what great nation is there that has such statutes and righteous judgments as are in all this law which I set before you this day? (Deut. 4:7–8)

God's people had the mind and heart of God expressed in the Law. They knew the conditions of the Law and their accountability before God. They knew God was holy and just. They knew He would not overlook sin. These people who were under Samuel's leadership had many centuries of witness to God's dealing with sin in His people. Their forefathers had been severely judged for their sin. God had not changed. And now *this* generation had to decide about sin in their lives, as those who inherited the covenant from their fathers.

GOD DEALS WITH HIS PEOPLE

The blessings, as well as the judgments of God, were inherited. No nation had ever been loved like Israel. They were God's special people. They knew this as they read God's instruction to them recorded in Deuteronomy:

> For you are a holy people to the LORD your God; the LORD your God has chosen you to be a people for Himself, a special treasure above all the peoples on the face of the earth. The LORD did not set His love on you nor choose you because you were more in number than any other people, for you were the least of all peoples; but because the LORD loves you, and because He would keep the oath which He swore to your fathers, the LORD has brought you out with a mighty hand, and redeemed you from the house of bondage, from the hand of Pharaoh king of Egypt.
>
> Therefore know that the LORD your God, He is God, the faithful God who keeps covenant and mercy for a thousand generations with those who love Him and keep His commandments; and He repays those who hate Him to their face, to destroy them. He will not be slack with him who hates Him; He will repay him to his face. Therefore you shall keep the commandment, the statutes, and the judgments which I command you today, to observe them. (7:6–11)

The glory of Israel was their God! There was no other. He alone was God! And this God had chosen them to be a "special treasure" for Himself. They in turn were to be holy and be a kingdom of priests. This carried with it not merely privilege, but responsibility and accountability. God was by nature Mercy and would be extremely patient and long-suffering with His people. At Moses' request God had "passed by" and revealed to him His name, or the essence of His nature:

> And the LORD passed before him and proclaimed, "The LORD, the LORD God, merciful and gracious, longsuffering, and abounding in goodness and

truth, keeping mercy for thousands, forgiving iniquity and transgression and sin . . ." (Ex. 34:6–7)

Moses never got over this gracious encounter with God. He then shared it earnestly with God's people, urging them to be faithful to the God who had entered into the covenant with them. He also, because of the stubbornness and sin in God's people, became a preeminent intercessor (see Ex. 34:9; Deut. 9:18–20, 25–29; 10:10), as did Samuel.

Because of the serious nature of this moment, and what it reveals about God, we will expand the truth, looking for this truth throughout the rest of the Bible. When any truth is seen clearly throughout the Bible, it must be taken very seriously for our own lives, and rigorously and ruthlessly applied.

The greater picture of this enormous tragedy was still spoken of by David, much later, as recorded in Psalm 78:56–64. It is worthwhile to quote this passage, even though it is long:

> Yet they tested and provoked the Most High God,
> And did not keep His testimonies,
> But turned back and acted unfaithfully like their fathers;
> They were turned aside like a deceitful bow.
> For they provoked Him to anger with their high places,
> And moved Him to jealousy with their carved images.
> When God heard this, He was furious,
> And greatly abhorred Israel,
> So that He forsook the tabernacle of Shiloh,
> The tent He had placed among men,
> And delivered His strength into captivity,
> And His glory into the enemy's hand.
> He also gave His people over to the sword,
> And was furious with His inheritance.
> The fire consumed their young men,

And their maidens were not given in marriage.

Their priests fell by the sword,

And their widows made no lamentation.

David himself was confronted by God for his sin. Having sinned grievously against both Bathsheba and her husband, Uriah, God sent another man, Nathan, to confront David for his sin against God. David had sinned against the full knowledge of the Law. Now, as a leader and king of his people, God had to make David realize how serious and extensive his sin was. Here is the indictment:

Then Nathan said to David, "You are the man! Thus says the LORD God of Israel: 'I anointed you king over Israel, and I delivered you from the hand of Saul. I gave you your master's house and your master's wives into your keeping, and gave you the house of Israel and Judah. And if that had been too little, I also would have given you much more! Why have you despised the commandment of the LORD, to do evil in His sight? You have killed Uriah the Hittite with the sword; you have taken his wife to be your wife, and have killed him with the sword of the people of Ammon. Now therefore, the sword shall never depart from your house, because you have despised Me, and have taken the wife of Uriah the Hittite to be your wife.'

"Thus says the LORD: 'Behold, I will raise up adversity against you from your own house; and I will take your wives before your eyes and give them to your neighbor, and he shall lie with your wives in the sight of this sun. For you did it secretly, but I will do this thing before all Israel, before the sun.'"

So David said to Nathan, "I have sinned against the LORD." And Nathan said to David, "The LORD also has put away your sin; you shall not die. However, because by this deed you have given great occasion to the enemies of the LORD to blaspheme, the child also who is born to you shall surely die." Then Nathan departed to his house. And the LORD struck the child that Uriah's wife bore to David, and it became ill. (2 Sam. 12:7–15)

God reminded David of His faithfulness to him. It was God Himself who had chosen him and anointed him king. In the eyes of God, David's sin was, in fact, despising God. This sin of David would affect his entire family and all of Israel all the days of his life. David's sin caused the enemies of God to blaspheme.

What did God have in mind when He told David that he had "despised" Him in sinning so grievously? It is important to know, because this is how God looks upon us when we sin. Sin is always against God. It is rebellion against God and all He has revealed (see Isa. 63:10; Lam. 3:42). Sin is a matter of the heart toward God (see Deut. 30:17; Jer. 3:10; Heb. 3:10). First John 3:4–6 states that sin is lawlessness, or choosing to act contrary to what God has commanded. In other words, to choose to sin is to choose to "despise God."

> **To choose to sin is to choose to "despise God."**

David knew this painfully when, realizing his sin, he cried out to God, "Against You, You only, have I sinned, and done this evil in Your sight" (Ps. 51:4).

David knew all sin was against God, and that it affected his relationship with God. This is why his cry is so deep and thorough in Psalm 51, using such phrases as:

- "blot out my transgressions" (v. 1)

- "wash me thoroughly from my iniquity" (v. 2)

- "cleanse me from my sin" (v. 2)

- "my sin is always before me" (v. 3)

- "purge me" (v. 7)

- "wash me" (v. 7)

- "make me hear joy and gladness" (v. 8)

- "hide Your face from my sins" (v. 9)

- "create in me a clean heart, O God" (v. 10)

- "renew a steadfast spirit within me" (v. 10)

- "do not cast me away from Your presence" (v. 11)

- "do not take Your Holy Spirit from me" (v. 11)

- "restore to me the joy of Your salvation" (v. 12)

- "uphold me by Your generous Spirit" (v. 12)

- "deliver me from the guilt of bloodshed" (v. 14)

Then he cried out in full recognition of God's requirement for repentance: "The sacrifices of God are a broken spirit, a broken and a contrite heart—These, O God, You will not despise" (Ps. 51:17).

He also knew that his sin was done "in [God's] sight" (v. 4). Whatever God did next, David knew it was right and loving and just, for he cried out in his prayer of repentance, "that You may be found just when You speak, and blameless when You judge" (v. 4).

Then David added, with transparent honesty before God, "Behold, You desire truth in the inward parts, and in the hidden part You will make me to know wisdom" (Ps. 51:6).

Here is a man who:

- knew God thoroughly

- had a heart like God

- knew God could withdraw His active, working presence from him, and be perfectly just in doing so

- knew that repentance was absolute and on God's terms

- rested everything on his honesty before God

- understood God's love and mercy toward him.

All this neither Eli, his sons, King Saul, nor Israel ever acknowledged. But forgiveness always rested and depended on this kind of repentance toward God.

How many of God's people today consider adultery, which so often results in death to families, as in fact "despising God"? And how many are ready for God to deal with them severely enough to restore in them His name among His people? The way in which God dealt with David's sin (as He did with Eli) would create a godly fear in the hearts of God's people all the days of their lives and act as a deterrent to their sins. Not only that, David's sin would be known and read by God's people to the end of time and become a deterrent to sin for many.

NEW TESTAMENT PICTURE OF ICHABOD

But this entire truth about Ichabod—*the glory has departed*—is seen even more clearly in the New Testament. The writer of Hebrews warned those to whom he was writing with these words:

> For if we sin willfully after we have received the knowledge of the truth, there no longer remains a sacrifice for sins, but a certain fearful expectation of judgment, and fiery indignation which will devour the adversaries. Anyone who has rejected Moses' law dies without mercy on the testimony of two or three witnesses. Of how much worse punishment, do you suppose, will he be thought worthy who has trampled the Son of God underfoot, counted the blood of the covenant by which he was sanctified a common thing, and insulted the Spirit of grace? For we know Him who said, *"Vengeance is Mine, I will repay,"* says the Lord. And again, *"The LORD*

will judge His people." It is a fearful thing to fall into the hands of the living God. (Heb. 10:26–31)

Let's look further at this Scripture from the New Testament.

First, God is speaking to *His* people! His people are a covenant people. They have been given a full understanding of God's conditions for entering this covenant! They know in detail all that God requires of them—in covenant. Under Jesus' lordship, God's people have in their hands *all* that He has commanded. He spoke some of His commands over and over again. God preserved for us four separate accounts—Matthew, Mark, Luke, and John. We are without excuse when we sin. In addition, God has given us the Spirit of Truth to teach us all things.

Second, when we continue to sin and disobey what He has commanded, after knowledge of the truth, there remains nothing more God can do except to carry out the conditions of His covenant and discipline or judge us. He will not be mocked. He will make certain we experience the fruit of our choices.

Third, He gives us a reminder of how God dealt with His people under Moses when He first gave the covenant privilege to His chosen people. God's judgment was severe and certain on all who disobeyed. Then came those fearful words for us! We have much more knowledge than those of Moses' day. We have the fullest revelation of God possible to man. We have Jesus!

Fourth, he describes how God looks on our sin. Hebrews 10:29 tells us that in continuing to sin after we have God's full revelation and the knowledge of truth, we have:

1. "trampled the Son of God underfoot";

2. "counted the blood of the covenant by which [each of us] was sanctified a common thing"; and

3. "insulted the Spirit of grace."

Then the writer adds a solemn quote from the Old Testament: "'Vengeance is Mine, I will repay,' says the Lord. And again, 'The LORD will judge His people'" (v. 30). He then concludes with a word of testimony, "It is a fearful thing to fall into the hands of the living God" (v. 31).

It is indeed a fearful thing "to fall into the hands of the living God"! This truth was written (and no doubt constantly spoken) to the churches of the New Testament times. This truth was experienced by Eli and all of Israel. It is once again desperately needed for God's people today! God is just as serious about sin in the corporate life of His people today as at any time in history. His covenant people today, the churches, are His primary means for taking His name and His great salvation to all the peoples of the world. As go His people, so will go His redemptive activity in the world. Eternity is still in the balance, and it is still true today. God is saying He is not willing that any should perish (see 2 Peter 3:9).

THE NATURE OF GOD

Here, then, is a very serious revelation of the nature of God, and His attitude toward sin! When His people sin, and continue to sin, after they have the knowledge of the truth, "there no longer remains a sacrifice for sins, but a certain fearful expectation of judgment, and fiery indignation" (Heb. 10:26–27).

Thus, both the Old and New Testaments bear witness to this side of the nature of God, especially in His relationship with *His* people.

Eli, God's leader for His people, had failed to teach the ways of God to the people, including his own children. Neither did he correct them when he knew they were not heeding the commands of God in the Law (see 1 Sam. 2:29). Therefore, Samuel had to deliver this evaluation by God on Eli's life:

95

> In that day I will perform against Eli all that I have spoken concerning his house, from beginning to end. For I have told him that I will judge his house forever for the iniquity which he knows, because his sons made themselves vile, and he did not restrain them. And therefore I have sworn to the house of Eli that the iniquity of Eli's house shall not be atoned for by sacrifice or offerings forever. (1 Sam. 3:12–14)

When our children are no longer taught, they tend to go astray, depart from the intimate relationship with God, and sin against Him. The longer they go untaught and uncorrected, the more they sin, and finally there comes God's, "Too late! Judgment has come upon you!"

Jesus, of all people, knew this thoroughly. He was constantly grieved by the lack of response to His presence and His testimony. John the Baptist had cried out faithfully, "Repent! For the kingdom of heaven is at hand!" (Matt. 3:2). No one could have been more impassioned or clear than John. Some responded immediately and with all their hearts. Others put off their decision, and still others rejected it outright. John was preparing the way for Jesus. Then came Jesus, and He, too, preached, "Repent, for the kingdom of heaven is at hand" (Matt. 4:17). God's people responded in the same way they had responded to John and to all those God had sent them. Jesus continued to preach with passion and even tears! They still would not hear and repent. Finally, with tears, Jesus cried out as He saw Jerusalem and knew the end was near. In fact the time had come to God's people of His day, and He said,

> If you had known, even you, especially in this your day, the things that make for your peace! But now they are hidden from your eyes. For days will come upon you when your enemies will build an embankment around you, surround you and close you in on every side, and level you, and your children within you, to the ground; and they will not leave in

you one stone upon another, because you did not know the time of your visitation. (Luke 19:42–44)

It was too late! Judgment had come upon them, and they would be destroyed! This is seen clearly as Jesus announced to God's people, in Luke 19:41 and following, "Too late! Judgment has come upon you, and you are going to be destroyed!" Again, in Revelation 2:1 and following, the living, risen Christ announced to the church at Ephesus, "Nevertheless I have this against you, that you have left your first love. Remember therefore from where you have fallen; repent and do the first works, or else I will come to you quickly and remove your lampstand from its place—unless you repent" (Rev. 2:4–5).

Once again, in the final book of the Bible, Revelation, God was clearly speaking to His covenant people. He now was addressing them as they were living out this covenant in the local churches. Here He has sent word through John to seven of the churches in Asia Minor. I have felt He was writing to Ephesus, the mother church, and her six mission churches. Every church is created by God and built by Jesus Christ and indwelt by His Holy Spirit. They are *His!* He gave them a love relationship with Himself, and He gave them the continuing conditions for remaining in this covenant. To fail to be faithful was even more serious for them than for His people in the Old Testament. The greatness of God's salvation was at stake. The redeeming of a lost world was at stake. His name and His eternal purpose were at stake. So He reminded these churches that they were to repent and remember their call and return to their "first love." If they did not, it would be over for them. God would "remove their lampstand"—their very existence (see Rev. 2:5).

THE SERIOUSNESS OF SIN

I have noticed, painfully, that the leaders of many churches fail to teach God's people about the seriousness of sin in the body of Christ. If a staff member sins grievously, his or her sin is often "dealt with in private." It is hidden from the people, and therefore the people are denied the teaching from the leaders about the seriousness of sin in their lives. The leaders say to themselves, "If we bring this sin out in the open to deal with it, we will disturb, and may lose, too many people. We can't afford to lose the people!" Thus, I believe, these leaders are perpetuating in our day the sin of failing to teach God's people about sin as God sees it, and God's people continue in sin to their destruction. God's name is at stake before God's people and before a watching world.

God constantly commanded that His people be taught. The Levites were assigned to teach God's people. Eli was a priest for God's people. There is no evidence he taught God's people the intimate relationship with God that the Law provided. The people had simply practiced the activity without the relationship with God, and their hearts departed from Him. They no longer loved Him and obeyed Him. They certainly did not fear Him. This four-hundred-year period of the judges was summed up simply: "Everyone did what was right in his own eyes" (Judg. 17:6; 21:25; see Deut. 12:8). This created spiritual anarchy and a loss of the corporate obedience that the covenant called for.

In some ways we are nearing "spiritual anarchy" in our own day, with each individual encouraged to find his own personal spiritual gift and ministry and go off and do it. This comes at a time when ignorance of God's Word seems to be at a high and increasing rate. We read the books of men who do not necessarily press us back to the Scriptures, but entertain us and encourage a strong affirming of *self*. Jesus told us to "deny self" and submit all to Him as Lord. The corporate covenant with God is almost nonexistent. There is little teaching, instructing, or warning of God's people.

Let us continue to examine further this crucial moment when the glory of God "departed from Israel!"

Jesus told us to "deny self" and submit all to Him as Lord.

Not only did God allow His ark to go into captivity to the enemies of His people, but this captivity was not for a short duration. His people lamented after God for twenty long years (see 1 Sam. 7:2). God is serious about sin in the corporate life of His people. This is because they are living out their lives as a covenant people of God, *before a watching world!* His name is at stake, the fear of Him is at stake, and ultimately His eternal purpose for the redemption of the world is at stake. This is just as true today as in any time during the Old and New Testaments. When God's people do not take seriously their sin against God, it can be, for them, "too late!"

Over the years I have witnessed this truth in people's lives. When a believer will not repent, after many attempts to restore him [or her], I have watched God deal with him severely. And when God does, too often those around this person fail to "get the message" from what God does. I have seen churches act in a very godless manner before their watching world, and they died. God "removed their lampstand" (their presence) from before the world. I have personally pleaded with some churches in this matter, without success, and those churches "died" and are no longer in existence. I have warned pastors and other leaders of this very truth. Many have heeded the Scriptures, repented, and now have a very productive ministry. Others did not. They even got angry at any suggestion of sin or repentance! The ones who did not repent are no longer in the ministry. Some never connected their sin with what God did next. They cried over their sins, but never did repent. They *said* they had repented, but to those who knew them and the Scriptures, it was clearly evident that they had not repented. Today, their lives are in ruins, and their ministries have ended. Too often, their families also are no longer serving their Lord.

Should this truth not be a "present wake-up call" to all of us? If we know we have sinned, and merely sense we have repented, but there is little or no evidence of God's restoring us to His favor, we must return to God and His Word, *until we see clearly His hand of blessing returning upon us*. If we are right with God in our covenant relationship, He *will* be blessing us.

However, God can discipline His children for an extended period of time, as He did here with Israel (twenty long years). Later, when God finally judged Jerusalem and Judah, He placed them in bondage in Babylon for seventy years (see Jer. 25:9–12). God may restore His people sooner than this if they repent. But He may linger and delay His restoration, giving His people time to realize more thoroughly the seriousness of their sin. God was not their servant; they were His servants, but they had hearts that were set in disobedience and rebellion to Him. He does not violate their responsibility to make right choices, but He does often seek to influence them toward right choices. And ultimately He holds them responsible for those decisions.

This brings us to another extremely important *defining moment* in the life of Israel, and the life of Samuel. The Scripture simply says, "Then Samuel spoke to all the house of Israel" (1 Sam 7:3). But it had taken the hand of God being withdrawn from them for *twenty years!* With God, often there is no quick restoration. It depends on the nature and extent of the sin, and the context of the sin. But eventually God once again will speak to His people and guide them carefully and clearly back into the covenant relationship with Himself. He did it to Israel, through Samuel. Samuel was once again God's instrument to speak to His people. Samuel was very specific in what God required of His people for them to return, and for Him to accept their return to Him. It is never on our terms, only God's terms. Here is where there must be a slow, careful, and purposeful study of 1 Samuel 7:2–17.

SEVEN

THE SPIRIT OF THE LORD CAME

Call upon Me in the day of trouble;
I will deliver you, and you shall glorify Me.
Psalm 50:15

Then the men of Kirjath Jearim came and took the ark of the LORD, and brought it into the house of Abinadab on the hill, and consecrated Eleazar his son to keep the ark of the LORD. So it was that the ark remained in Kirjath Jearim a long time; it was there twenty years. And all the house of Israel lamented after the LORD. Then Samuel spoke to all the house of Israel, saying, "If you return to the LORD with all your hearts, then put away the foreign gods and the Ashtoreths from among you, and prepare your hearts for the LORD, and serve Him only; and He will deliver you from the hand of the Philistines." . . . And Samuel judged Israel all the days of his life. (1 Sam. 7:1–3, 15)

I AM A LONG WAY FROM THE INCARNATION of this message in my life. One thing about the Lord Jesus—He was the incarnation of everything He taught and preached. What He taught and what He spoke was from His life, for He was the message. Jesus intends that there should never be a message that comes from any of our hearts or mouths that is not incarnated in our lives. God says that if you say one thing and live another then you are filled with hypocrisy. God hates hypocrisy. Too often we believe anything is acceptable to God as long as it is based on Scripture. We forget that the proclaimer needs to be the incarnation of the message he preaches. For example, do not preach on forgiveness if you do not have forgiveness in your heart and are not openly practicing forgiveness in your life.

> **Too often we believe anything is acceptable to God as long as it is based on Scripture.**

It is critically important that you understand the character of the person who leads God's people in corporate repentance and revival. When God's people cry out, "We have sinned against God!"—not just anybody can guide the people of God who recognize they are under conviction of sin to know what to do next. But Samuel did. And there is a reason why he did.

DISOBEDIENCE

Chapter 7 of 1 Samuel is a *defining moment* for both Samuel and God's people. They would once again encounter God and His ways. They would experience God's severe judgment on the sin of disobedience. God had very strict commands concerning the ark of the covenant. No one was to look into it, except those whom God specifically permitted.

This matter of "looking on God" was given as a warning to His people when the covenant was first given. When Moses was invited by God to come into His presence on Mount Sinai, God told Moses to warn the people:

> "Also let the priests who come near the LORD consecrate themselves, lest the LORD break out against them." But Moses said to the LORD, "The people cannot come up to Mount Sinai; for You warned us, saying, 'Set bounds around the mountain and consecrate it.'" (Ex. 19:22–23)

Throughout the Old Testament, it was a serious and fatal sin to touch the glory of God, especially as symbolized by God's presence through the ark.

David felt the fear of the Lord when he saw Uzzah die for touching the ark (see 2 Sam. 6:6–11).

God kept instructing His people in the seriousness of their covenant relationship with Him. He was God and they were His people. They were to be holy. No casual or careless relationship with God was tolerated, for such behavior would encourage all of God's people to depart from Him and His covenant relationship with them. Now God once again would teach His people to obey Him, by judging careless behavior toward Him. Israel needed a deep renewal, or revival, in their relationship with God. Every "next generation" of God's people must return fully to the original covenant relationship with God.

> Then He struck the men of Beth Shemesh, because they had looked into the ark of the LORD. He struck fifty thousand and seventy men of the people, and the people lamented because the LORD had struck the people with a great slaughter. (1 Sam. 6:19)

In our day we will never see a mighty revival until we understand the ways of God. When someone sins against God it is serious with God. He may take the life of fifty thousand people simply because they looked into the ark. The evangelical community does not believe we serve the God we see revealed in the Scriptures, especially the Old Testament. We feel we can live any way we want and God will just forgive us regardless of what we have done. There is a major problem with that thinking. That is not the God revealed in the Bible.

Lest someone think that the God of the Old Testament dealt with sin, but the God of the New Testament only gives grace, and not judgment, saying "This is the Old Testament—we live under the New Testament!" I remind you that God is just as sensitive to the issue of sin in the New Testament as He is in the Old Testament.

Remember the warning of Jesus to those inquiring of Him about a tragic moment in their day. Jesus' reply was clear and vivid when He said,

> "Do you suppose that these Galileans were worse sinners than all other Galileans, because they suffered such things? I tell you, no; but unless you repent you will all likewise perish. Or those eighteen on whom the tower in Siloam fell and killed them, do you think that they were worse sinners than all other men who dwelt in Jerusalem? I tell you, no; but unless you repent you will all likewise perish." (Luke 13:2–5)

Later, Jesus said they had not heeded His warning and were all now going to perish under the judgment hand of God, His Father:

> Now as He drew near, He saw the city and wept over it, saying, "If you had known, even you, especially in this your day, the things that make for your peace! But now they are hidden from your eyes. For days will come upon you when your enemies will build an embankment around you, surround you and close you in on every side, and level you, and your children within you, to the ground; and they will not leave in you one stone upon another, because you did not know the time of your visitation." (Luke 19:41–44)

Remember, this actually took place in A.D. 70–72!

Jesus had pleaded with God's people and revealed not only the heart of the Father, but also His persistent love for them:

> O Jerusalem, Jerusalem, the one who kills the prophets and stones those who are sent to her! How often I wanted to gather your children together, as a hen gathers her brood under her wings, but you were not willing! See! Your house is left to you desolate; and assuredly, I say to you, you shall not see Me until the time comes when you say, "Blessed is He who comes in the name of the LORD!" (Luke 13:34–35)

This loving, even pleading, heart of God is consistent throughout the entire Bible and continues to this very day! No Christian should take sin lightly! God will begin a strong discipline with us to persuade us to forsake sin and return to Him quickly. The clearest picture of this heart of God is recorded in Hebrews.

And you have forgotten the exhortation which speaks to you as to sons:

> "My son, do not despise the chastening of the LORD,
> Nor be discouraged when you are rebuked by Him;
> For whom the LORD loves He chastens,
> And scourges every son whom He receives."

If you endure chastening, God deals with you as with sons; for what son is there whom a father does not chasten? But if you are without chastening, of which all have become partakers, then you are illegitimate and not sons. Furthermore, we have had human fathers who corrected us, and we paid them respect. Shall we not much more readily be in subjection to the Father of spirits and live? For they indeed for a few days chastened us as seemed best to them, but He for our profit, that we may be partakers of His holiness. Now no chastening seems to be joyful for the present, but painful; nevertheless, afterward it yields the peaceable fruit of righteousness to those who have been trained by it. (Heb. 12:5–11)

God had confronted Eli with the way he was treating his sons. He was honoring his sons more than God. Suddenly, in his old age, Eli realized that his sons were wicked. So he came to them and tried to instruct them, "If one man sins against another, God will judge him. But if a man sins against the LORD, who will intercede for him?" (1 Sam. 2:25). When he finished giving that instruction, the Bible says his sons paid no attention to Eli because God had determined to kill his sons. In other words, they could not have repented if they had wanted to. Just as Esau sought repentance with tears but could not find it (see Heb. 12:16–17), they likewise could not repent. We need to understand the ways of God. Again, some may say, "Well that is Old Testament." I respond by saying, "No, that is not Old Testament; that is a Holy God."

JUDGMENT

When you cry out for revival, you must be ready for the absolute judgment of God on your sin! However, too many today do not believe God will judge our sin. It is revealed when you hear this statement: "It doesn't matter what you have done, God will forgive you anyway." That is adulterating the Word of God, and it causes the people of God to sin. People believe God will forgive them of whatever they have done without any repentance. That is not so. If you have no understanding of what God means by repenting, then do not expect God to forgive any and every sin you simply confess to Him. Confession is not repentance! It merely acknowledges that what God sees is true. Confession, if from the heart, must be followed by deep and genuine repentance. Then God forgives!

Too often we set our own standard for repentance.

Too often we set our own standard for repentance and say, "God forgave me because I asked Him to." Where in the world did that thinking come from? These people with Samuel had sinned against God. It does not matter whether you think it is sin or not. If God thinks it is sin, you will experience the consequences. Looking into the ark? What is wrong with that? Well, let God show you. More than fifty thousand died because of that act of disobedience. Do you think that would leave the impression that it was sin? The people of Beth Shemesh did believe and cried out,

"Who is able to stand before this holy LORD God? And to whom shall it go up from us?" (1 Sam. 6:20). So they sent messengers to the inhabitants of Kirjath Jearim, saying, "The Philistines have brought back the ark of the LORD; come down and take it up with you." Then the men of Kirjath Jearim came and took the ark of the LORD, and brought it into the house of Abinadab on the hill, and consecrated Eleazar his son to keep the ark of the LORD. So it was that the ark remained in Kirjath Jearim a long time; it was there twenty years. And all the house of Israel lamented after the LORD. (1 Sam. 6:21–7:2)

This is a solemn truth about the ways of God.

You are simply seeing another of the ways of God. God does not respond merely because we pray. God responds out of His sovereign ways that are consistent with His holy nature. How long would it have taken God to return the ark to the people of God? He could have done it in a day! Why did God let the ark be out of the presence of the people of God for twenty long years? Why did He let the people of God lament after God for twenty years with nothing happening? They had lost the sense of the presence of God. They had somehow felt that they owned God and, if they prayed, He was obligated to respond. They needed to return to God in deepest repentance. God knew their hearts and knew it would take time.

Will God let us pray for twenty years for revival and delay it? Yes! But when His people become the people He can give revival to, then God will sovereignly bring revival in his own timing. We automatically assume that the basic condition for God acting is our prayer. It is not! You cannot receive the incredible empowering of God without prayer, but that is not the only condition of it. Then, in the middle of this situation comes Samuel.

Remember, there was no open revelation for the people of God (see 1 Sam. 3:1). There was no word for the people. The sin of Eli and his sons had disoriented the people of God to a relationship to God. Even the elders did not know what to do. They sinned, not even knowing they were sinning.

When the Philistines defeated the children of Israel the elders said, "What has God done?" God's basic response was, "I am glad you asked, but I do not think you really want the answer!"

It is the sin of the people that disoriented them to God. They were the people of God, with the covenant of God and the Law of God and the testimonies and statutes of God. It was not that they were not a covenant people. They had moved from a relationship to religion. That shift was a movement away from God. They no longer recognized God's voice when He spoke. When God acted, they did not realize it was Him. They asked the right question but did not expect the answer they received. They wanted to know why God had let these things come upon them. They thought if they would just get the ark and take it into battle that would make them secure. Evangelicals have their little "arks" they take into battle as well. It makes sense to us that God will hear the evangelicals. Not necessarily. If sin runs rampant in the church of evangelicals, God will not hear (you can count on it). There will be silence from God. He will come into our lives and our churches and allow captivity of our most sacred things.

Judgment fell! The elders, with human reasoning now distorted by sin, were the ones who said to take the ark and that would save them. God let the Philistines capture the ark, but the ark put the Philistines in greater distress. God took the ark from the Israelites for twenty years, to somehow cause someone to say there must be something wrong.

REPENTANCE

From the time I was a little boy I have prayed for revival in Canada. My uncle worked with Jonathan Goforth in China and was in the great Shantung revival. As I have been studying these passages it has been as though God wanted me to ask Him why I have prayed so long with little evidence of national revival. Each one, seriously praying for revival, must ask this question. But we must wait for God's answer. His answer came in Samuel's day—through Samuel.

I want you to see Samuel's simple and clear answer and what God did in answer to his cry as he interceded for the people before God.

Here is revealed the corporate nature of revival. You must understand that all the individual renewal for repentance and awakening is never a substitute for corporate revival and corporate repentance. We are a covenant people. We are a corporate people. We are a people who belong to God and to one another. God does not just play favorites with individuals to bring renewal and not touch the people of God. All the way through the Bible, including Pentecost, revival came on the people of God, and in the New Testament, the churches.

Here is a *defining moment*:

> Then Samuel spoke to all the house of Israel, saying, "If you return to the LORD with all your hearts, then put away the foreign gods and the Ashtoreths from among you, and prepare your hearts for the LORD, and serve Him only; and He will deliver you from the hand of the Philistines." So the children of Israel put away the Baals and the Ashtoreths, and served the LORD only. And Samuel said, "Gather all Israel to Mizpah, and I will pray to the LORD for you." So they gathered together at Mizpah, drew water, and poured it out before the LORD. And they fasted that day, and said there, "We have sinned against the LORD." And Samuel judged the children of Israel at Mizpah. Now when the Philistines heard that the children of Israel had gathered together at Mizpah, the lords of the Philistines went up against Israel. And when the children of Israel heard of it, they were afraid of the Philistines. (1 Sam. 7:3–7)

Do you know that God's people are still afraid of the Philistines? When we are in a corporate gathering and saying all kinds of things against the enemy, we feel fairly secure. That is, until the Philistines hear about our gathering and start to organize against us. We need to identify who our Philistines are. They will gather when they see the people of God gathering together. It is always a good thing for us also, when you see the Philistines gather, that you corporately say, "We have sinned!"

You do not need to say that Hollywood, Washington, or the gays and lesbians have gathered against us. But God's people must cry out, "We have sinned against God!" We must let the holy presence of God tell us what it is that we have done that is so offensive to God. Do not just say that God has told you to confess your sin but you really do not know what you have done. This is too often the evangelical thing to do. You may pray that you have sinned against God, but He wants you to name what you have done. Stay before God until you know what you have done. When God is done with you, then you can make the connection between the condition of your land and the sin of the people of God.

As go the people of God in their relationship to God, so goes the nation. September 11, 2001, was God speaking to His people. He was saying that we have sinned. God was announcing that He was beginning to withdraw His hedge of protection on our land. But it seems that the only people in America who have never gotten His message are God's people. Look now at many bulletins and orders of worship and compare them with the first Sunday after September 11, 2001, and most will not show a difference. You would never know that 9/11 ever happened. Much of the world has changed, but not the people of God. We do not believe the problem has to do with our condition. Yet sin runs through the churches across our land. Divorce and broken relationships reveal that we have forgotten our assigned ministry of reconciliation (see 2 Cor. 5:17–20).

When something happens in our land we act like the Israelites, wondering why God let this happen to us.

So Samuel stood up after twenty years of the people lamenting and told the people to respond to God with all their hearts. If they would respond, God would take care of the Philistines.

HOW TO RETURN

Look once again at the clarity and simplicity of God's message to His people, through His servant Samuel (1 Sam. 7:3):

1. *"If you return to the Lord . . ."* Sin always separates us from God and His activity among us. Isaiah proclaimed this situation clearly:

> Behold, the LORD's hand is not shortened,
>
> That it cannot save;
>
> Nor His ear heavy,
>
> That it cannot hear.
>
> But your iniquities have separated you from your God;
>
> And your sins have hidden His face from you,
>
> So that He will not hear.
>
> For your hands are defiled with blood,
>
> And your fingers with iniquity;
>
> Your lips have spoken lies,
>
> Your tongue has muttered perversity.
>
> No one calls for justice,
>
> Nor does any plead for truth.
>
> They trust in empty words and speak lies;
>
> They conceive evil and bring forth iniquity. (Isa. 59:1–4)

   The only response acceptable to God was to forsake *sin* and return to Him without delay.

2. *"with all your hearts . . ."* God only accepts a total response. Our entire beings must return to Him, not merely a segment or part of our lives. He is God, and only our all is worthy of Him or acceptable to Him (see Deut. 6:4–9).

3. *"then put away the foreign gods and the Ashtoreths from among you . . ."*
   A "god" is anything we turn to when God told us to turn
   exclusively to Him. For He is honored only when we turn to Him
   for deliverance:

   > Call upon Me in the day of trouble;
   > I will deliver you, and you shall glorify Me. (Ps. 50:15)

   How much do we turn to the world (i.e., foreign gods) for
   finances, counsel, future projections, marketing, music,
   entertainment, success, or even leadership styles?

4. *"and prepare your hearts for the Lord . . ."* Here is where we often
   are woefully deficient and lacking. The hearts must be cleansed.
   Our minds must be clean (see Rom. 12:1–2), and our
   relationships must be restored. We must stand before God and let
   Him examine our hearts, reveal our real condition, and show us
   where and how we must return to Him with our hearts that are
   ready for Him.

   > Who may ascend into the hill of the LORD?
   > Or who may stand in His holy place?
   > He who has clean hands and a pure heart,
   > Who has not lifted up his soul to an idol,
   > Nor sworn deceitfully.
   > He shall receive blessing from the LORD,
   > And righteousness from the God of his salvation. (Ps. 24:3–5)

   This is what John the Baptist was sent to do among God's
   people. He was to "prepare the way of the LORD, make His paths
   straight" (Matt. 3:3). The way the Lord has marked out is the
   only acceptable way to Him.

While Annas and Caiaphas were high priests, the word of God came to John the son of Zacharias in the wilderness. And he went into all the region around the Jordan, preaching a baptism of repentance for the remission of sins, as it is written in the book of the words of Isaiah the prophet, saying:

> "The voice of one crying in the wilderness:
> 'Prepare the way of the LORD;
> Make His paths straight.
> Every valley shall be filled
> And every mountain and hill brought low;
> The crooked places shall be made straight
> And the rough ways smooth;
> And all flesh shall see the salvation of God.'" (Luke 3:2–6)

Zacharias, John the Baptist's father, also prophesied significantly of this preparation for the Lord.

> And you, child, will be called the prophet of the Highest;
> For you will go before the face of the Lord to prepare His ways,
> To give knowledge of salvation to His people
> By the remission of their sins,
> Through the tender mercy of our God,
> With which the Dayspring from on high has visited us;
> To give light to those who sit in darkness and the shadow of death,
> To guide our feet into the way of peace. (Luke 1:76–79)

5. *"and serve Him only . . ."* Him only! No divided heart!

> He who is not with Me is against Me, and he who does not gather with Me scatters abroad. (Matt. 12:30)

> No servant can serve two masters; for either he will hate the one and love the other, or else he will be loyal to the one and despise the other. You cannot serve God and mammon. (Luke 16:13)

Take time, right now, to examine your heart and life in the light of this Scripture and admonition of Samuel to God's people. This is crucial and can never be casual or careless.

PRAYER FOR THE PEOPLE OF GOD

> So the children of Israel said to Samuel, "Do not cease to cry out to the LORD our God for us, that He may save us from the hand of the Philistines." And Samuel took a suckling lamb and offered it as a whole burnt offering to the LORD. Then Samuel cried out to the LORD for Israel, and the LORD answered him. (1 Sam. 7:8–9)

First Samuel 7:8–9 is a very revealing moment about God's people in time of crisis. They looked immediately for someone who knew God and whom God knew intimately. If they found someone like this, they would ask him to pray for them and intercede before God on their behalf. They sensed that their deliverance from the Philistines rested on Samuel's prayer life! They had no confidence in their own prayers for twenty years but had all the evidence they needed that God heard Samuel's prayers. What a testimony to this faithful servant of God. But what an indictment on the elders and the people of God!

What do you do in times of serious crisis? What do you do when people cry out to you in their sin for you to pray for them and their safety? If we are not careful in our walks with God, we may very well simply let them experience the consequences of their sin—and they will, and severely, if we do not intercede.

Samuel knew his significant role before God for the people. He loved God and he loved His people, so he did what was required by God—he offered a whole burnt offering to the Lord (see Lev. 22:26–33) and "cried out to the LORD for Israel" (1 Sam. 7:9). Then comes a most significant affirming of Samuel by God before all God's people, "and the LORD answered him" (1 Sam. 7:9).

God answered Samuel's prayer by confusing the enemy, thus allowing Israel to defeat the Philistines.

Many of us want to cry out to God for revival, but we do not want to offer sin offerings to God. You must have a clean heart and a cleansed life. We know the Scripture that says, "The effective, fervent prayer of a righteous man avails much" (James 5:16), but we too often pay no attention to our righteousness before God. But remember, at that moment the survival of the people of God was at stake. Now it came down to one person! Thank God that they had observed the prayer life of Samuel. Do you have enough of a track record before God's people that they would call on you if a serious crisis came?

This may be a good time to place before you the solitary figures who have stood before God for His people, the figures whom God heard and then gave His people great deliverance (i.e., Rees Howells, Praying Hyde, David Brainard, George Mueller, and many ordinary people used of God in great revivals).

Our nation and our world are in serious spiritual and physical crisis. Where are the Samuels of God who will intercede? May it not be found in our day what is recorded in Ezekiel 22: "So I sought for a man among them who would make a wall, and stand in the gap before Me on behalf of the land, that I should not destroy it; but I found no one. Therefore I have poured out My indignation on them; I have consumed them with the fire of My wrath; and I have recompensed their deeds on their own heads," says the Lord GOD (vv. 30–31).

Now as Samuel was offering up the burnt offering, the Philistines drew near to battle against Israel. But the LORD thundered with a loud thunder upon the Philistines that day, and so confused them that they were over-come before Israel. (1 Sam. 7:10)

The Lord has a thousand ways to take care of the enemy. You do not have to instruct Him in what to do. He knows what will discomfort the enemy. It would not take God a week to put all the enemies in place. One blow from God will destroy all the enemies. But He has to have His people in a relationship with Him so that when He does do it, all the glory will go to God. He has to have His people undistracted by the world, and in covenant with Him.

We must have leaders who know what to do next when the people cry out that they have sinned. Leaders must know how to lead the people of God into corporate repentance in such a way that it is credible to God and to men.[1]

And the men of Israel went out of Mizpah and pursued the Philistines, and drove them back as far as below Beth Car. (1 Sam. 7:11)

Some of them could have at this moment said, "Look what *we* did." There will never come a time when there is a victory that you can say, "Look what *we* did." To keep God's people from pride and from touching the glory that belongs to God alone, "Samuel took a stone and set it up between Mizpah and Shen, and called its name Ebenezer, saying, 'Thus far the LORD has helped us'" (1 Sam. 7:12).

Ebenezer! This word is in our hymnbooks in such familiar hymns as *Come, Thou Fount of Every Blessing:*

Here I raise mine Ebenezer;
Hither by Thy help I'm come;
And I hope, by Thy good pleasure,
Safely to arrive at home . . .

Samuel was careful to leave a permanent legacy and physical reminder of the victory God wrought that day for His people. He took a stone and set it up between Mizpah and Shen. He called the stone Ebenezer, which means "stone of help."

What physical markers or reminders have you set up in your home for your children to know about the victories God has brought to you through prayer and deliverance? What about in your church? What about in your workplace? We would do well to remember Psalm 111:

> The works of the LORD are great,
> Studied by all who have pleasure in them. (v. 2)

> He has made His wonderful works to be remembered;
> The LORD is gracious and full of compassion. (v. 4)

Have you ever asked the question "Why is the hand of God not against the enemies of America?" Many ask for God to send a prophet. But that is God's last line of defense before judgment.

Some pastors say they cannot preach a message of repentance to the people because they would run him off. Why did God put pastors in churches anyway? Was it not to lead God's people to repent of their sin when they depart from Him? Jeremiah 23:22 says, "But if they had stood in My counsel, and had caused My people to hear My words, then they would have turned them from their evil way and from the evil of their doings." We are too often more concerned about the opinions of men than we are about God's Word and our obedience to Him.

Read again the awesome words of God in Revelation 1–3, especially His constant command to the "angel of the churches" (the pastors) to call their people to repentance. Everything with God rested upon repentance. It is just as true today. The enemies of God and His people press in on every side. We need courageous men of God to bring the age-old covenant message of

God to His people and return them in fear, brokenness, and repentance to God. Would it not be wonderful if community after community across the nation would say of us, "So the Philistines were subdued, and they did not come anymore into the territory of Israel. And the hand of the LORD was against the Philistines all the days of Samuel" (1 Sam. 7:13). We need to take back the land which the enemy has taken from us.

We need to take back the land which the enemy has taken from us.

Not only was the enemy defeated, but "the cities which the Philistines had taken from Israel were restored to Israel" (1 Sam. 7:14). We need to take back the land which the enemy has taken from us—the schools, the media, traditional family life, governmental halls, the courts, and other places our founding fathers dedicated to God for His glory. Pray to this end and be restored to God so He can do it through you and His people one more time!

> Then the cities which the Philistines had taken from Israel were restored to Israel, from Ekron to Gath; and Israel recovered its territory from the hands of the Philistines. Also there was peace between Israel and the Amorites. And Samuel judged Israel all the days of his life. He went from year to year on a circuit to Bethel, Gilgal, and Mizpah, and judged Israel in all those places. But he always returned to Ramah, for his home was there. There he judged Israel, and there he built an altar to the LORD. (1 Sam. 7:14–17)

What a beautiful summary of the remaining days of Samuel's life. But the people never seemed to learn from their mistakes.

It is not enough for one person to repent, though that is good. All the people need to repent. It is not enough for a few deacons or staff members to repent—they all need to repent. When a whole church cries out to God, under the guidance of the Word of God and the faithful sharing of the servant of God, God will respond.

Do you see the manifest presence of God in your church?

Do not say everything is all right when it is not. Let God encounter you, and pray that His encounter is not in such judgments as Israel experienced during the life of Samuel!

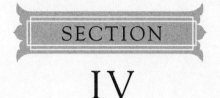

DEFINING MOMENTS

*Then all the elders of Israel gathered together and came to
Samuel at Ramah, and said to him, "Look, you are old,
and your sons do not walk in your ways.
Now make us a king to judge us like all the nations."*

1 SAMUEL 8:4–5

EIGHT

ISRAEL DEMANDS A KING

Heed the voice of the people in all that they say to you;
for they have not rejected you, but they have rejected Me,
that I should not reign over them.

1 Samuel 8:7

CHAPTER 8 OF THE FIRST BOOK OF SAMUEL
reveals a solemn truth: The sin of the leaders is
dramatic in both its short- and long-term effects.
When Samuel was old, his sons sinned grievously
against God and the people of God. Several important truths are quickly evident, and should be carefully and diligently remembered for our own lives:

> **The sin of the**
> **leaders is dramatic**
> **in both its**
> **short- and**
> **long-term effects.**

1. The leader who sins does not seek the Lord or His commands for
   himself or God's people. The result is that disaster follows at God's
   command.

2. The sin of leaders brings about sin in the lives of other key
   leaders, here called "elders"—they also do not seek the Lord,
   and guide the people of God into folly and destruction.

3. Inevitably the people of God make disastrous decisions by not
   seeking the Lord but instead merely doing what their leaders tell

them to do. All the people of God then make a corporate decision that offends and even angers God. God's anger results in a decision to not follow His plans to bless His people, but to discipline, or even judge, His people. This moment, both for Samuel and for the people of Israel, was without a doubt a defining moment. Their decision would affect the people of God for the rest of time!

Are there such defining moments inherently found in the midst of our decisions? There are! Therefore, every decision must be made in the conscious presence of God, and clearly in the center of the known will of God!

There was a time in my life when I realized that I was being passed over for (what I felt were) significant leadership positions. I had to make a serious decision. I could either choose to become bitter and resentful against my coworkers, or I could clearly accept this as the will of God, knowing that He was directing my life at that moment. I chose to honor God and believe that He was indeed involved in those decisions. Since that time, it has been obvious that God was involved and that He has taken me to other places of leadership in His purposes. God also has preserved my children from being resentful toward God's people over the incident.

I have seen over the years that many pastors' children become hurt and resentful at how their dads were treated, resulting in their leaving the church or at least refusing to let God call them into the ministry. All five of our children did respond to God's call on their lives to enter ministry, and are serving faithfully and well to this day. One moment of decision in my life can have a tragic or blessed effect on others. It is a choice I make regularly.

The corporate decisions of the leaders of God's people can also be very significant! First Samuel 8:4–5 indicates this moment: "Then all the elders of Israel gathered together and came to Samuel at Ramah, and said to him, 'Look, you are old, and your sons do not walk in your ways. Now make us a king to judge us like all the nations.'" This was a corporate decision, and a tragic and *defining moment* for the people of God! What follows next is so very instructive, not only for Samuel, but for any leader of God's people at any time. Samuel was deeply hurt, and even frightened. He knew God. He knew the ways of God and feared for the safety and future of his people—and rightly so! But as God's servant, Samuel did what he should do immediately—he "prayed to the LORD" (1 Sam. 8:6). He was deeply grieved and displeased! He trembled before God at the leaders' decision.

When God's people make a wrong choice, request that their choice be honored, and do not listen to reason from the Lord, it is crucial for the leader to go to the Lord in prayer before he does anything in response. A leader must have the mind of God. What God does next may surprise you as it did Samuel. God said: "Heed the voice of the people in all that they say to you; for they have not rejected you, but they have rejected Me, that I should not reign over them" (1 Sam. 8:7). This is an amazing and even disturbing moment for Samuel. But God always has a bigger picture than we do. Listen to God's perspective on His people: "According to all the works which they have done since the day that I brought them up out of Egypt, even to this day—with which they have forsaken Me and served other gods—so they are doing to you also" (1 Sam. 8:8).

GOD DOES NOT ABANDON HIS PEOPLE!

God observed that from the very day He delivered them from bondage in Egypt His people had rebelled against Him, rejected Him as "King" over them, and worshiped and served other gods. What an indictment! Yet He did not destroy them. What incredible mercy and grace and love! Certainly God gave them undeserved and unmerited favor. This shows the nature and the ways of our God. He does not reject the people of His covenant. They may reject Him, but He will not reject or abandon them. He will discipline them, and often very severely, but He does not abandon His people. A watching world secures their understanding of God by the way God relates to His people, especially what He does with them when they sin against Him.

This is a moment for careful reflection. How do we respond to God's people when they do not live up to our expectations or do not do what we think they ought to do? Too often I have heard God's people say something like this: "My church is sinning against God in the decision(s) they are making. I think they are wrong. If this is the way they are going to act, I am going to leave this church and find another church." If God does not abandon His people, how can we abandon them? How can we act so carelessly against His people? Leaving a church family that we do not agree with can greatly hurt or hinder that church and harm what God wants to do through our lives as a part of that body. Somehow we need a greater trust in God, to whom we belong. God will work with His people and, if need be, discipline them— but we better not play God in their lives by the way we treat them. Do what Samuel did—*pray to the Lord!* Then wait to hear from His perspective, and be available to Him to work among His people for God's glory!

A further word—to the elders, or deacons, or other leaders—should be considered. In the mind of God the primary assignment of His leader is to maintain unity in the people of God (the local church body). Too often those who are to keep the peace and unity are the very ones who lead God's people into seriously wrong decisions, which cost them dearly. God will hold these leaders accountable! When you are about to take action in leading God's people, always ask the question, "Will what I am suggesting to God's people lead to greater unity and greater honor to God, or will it be divisive and hurtful to the cause of Christ and His kingdom?"

Use the Scriptures extensively, and lead the people to *come together* to pray and seek the will of God in the matter. He *is* present, and He *will* guide you safely through any situation. I have heard some leaders respond to this line of thinking with, "You don't know our church and our situation. Our people will not respond to God the way you are suggesting!"

My only response is, "But I don't think you know well enough the God of the Scriptures. Is there anything too hard for Him? Is your church the first one He is unable to help and change and bless?"

THE CULTURE AROUND US

But there is also another very instructive factor present in this *defining moment* for Israel. Whether they knew it or not, they had been deeply affected by the culture around them. They had come to long for the ways of the world: "Now make us a king to judge us like all the nations" (1 Sam. 8:5). God had clearly told them they were not to be like all the other nations. He would be their God, and they would be His people. God would make His people so qualitatively different from the other nations that they would display before the world what He was like. He would remind them that He had always led them into battle against their enemies, and they always won the battles. Even after Samuel delivered all the words of God to the people, "the people refused to obey the voice of Samuel; and they said, 'No, but we will have a king over us, that we also may be like all the nations, and that our king may judge us and go out before us and fight our battles'" (1 Sam. 8:19–20).

Then came a fateful word from the Lord: "So the LORD said to Samuel, 'Heed their voice, and make them a king'" (1 Sam. 8:22). God's granting their request did not at all mean that God looked with favor on them and was blessing them. It was the exact opposite. God was angry with them as He granted their request. Later, through the prophet Hosea, God recalled this very moment and declared,

> O Israel, you are destroyed,
> But your help is from Me.
> I will be your King;
> Where is any other,

127

That he may save you in all your cities?
And your judges to whom you said,
"Give me a king and princes"?
I gave you a king in My anger,
And took him away in My wrath. (Hos. 13:9–11)

I have all too often observed a church allowing a "church split" to occur. Many of those people believed that because they were able to accomplish the split, they were experiencing the blessing of God. Those same people who left the original body of believers had the audacity to come before God the very next Sunday in corporate prayer, and pray, "O God, bless us today in this place!" There is another Scripture, describing how God responds to a people's request that is made in sin:

They soon forgot His works;
They did not wait for His counsel,
But lusted exceedingly in the wilderness,
And tested God in the desert.
And He gave them their request,
But sent leanness into their soul. (Ps. 106:13–15)

What a *defining moment* for the people of God! Yet they did not know the severity of the consequences, nor did they know that it was sin—until God later showed them the seriousness of their action and the fact that it was sin. Only then would they cry out to God in repentance, but it would be too late, and God would not hear them (see 1 Sam. 8:18). God did not respond—in order to help them become painfully aware of their sin and the severity of the consequences from His perspective. Further, God's purpose is for a watching world to know of His holiness by how He deals with His people. God's people made a fatal exchange when they asked for a king—like the world had—instead of having God to be their King.

A tragic mistake, made too often in our day, is the desire by God's people (often led by their leaders) to be like the world around them. They exchange their worship styles for ones that attract the world. Their youth music is exchanged to be more like the world. Often even their dress code is to attract the world around them. There is seemingly an age-old desire to be like the world around us, and to reject the godly patterns that He has blessed up until their day. I know that this is a sensitive topic in our day, but I would urge you to discuss this carefully, with an open Bible, asking God to teach and instruct you. See if you are asking for what the world has and if what you are asking for can be a fatal exchange for Him. Are you now turning to the world for what God asked you to receive from Him?

> **Are you now turning to the world for what God asked you to receive from Him?**

THE MYSTERY OF GOD

If you read and study the eighth chapter of 1 Samuel, you must wonder about the mystery of God seen here. It is mysterious that God would grant them their request, knowing that it was sin against Him; knowing also that it would be a fatal exchange with dire consequences. Do not presume that the permission of God is the will of God! He may send leanness into your soul also (see Ps. 106:15), knowing the stubbornness of your heart toward His will or His ways. I have known some sincere believers who insist that God delights in their persistence in making requests to Him. They leave the impression that God is pleased if they "keep on keeping on," even insisting that God grant them their request. There must be a balance in such praying. God's will, revealed in His Word, should never be overridden by your desires. Nor should you insist on your will once God has revealed His will. It is crucial that you wait before the Lord until His will is clearly known. Paul prayed three times for a "thorn in the flesh" to be removed, and finally

God said, "No!" There is something about God's power that Paul would never know by experience unless that weakness remained. Jesus seems to have earnestly prayed three times in Gethsemane for God to "remove this cup from Me." God's answer was, "No! I cannot save You and save the world too!" In both instances the final word was, "Not My will, but Thine be done!" The Israelites should never have insisted on their will over God's will. He granted it, in anger, and it affected them permanently.

Thus was set in motion a people with a king, like all the other nations. Now God instructed Samuel to tell them what the characteristics of a king would be. Samuel stood before the people and said:

> This will be the behavior of the king who will reign over you: He will take your sons and appoint them for his own chariots and to be his horsemen, and some will run before his chariots. He will appoint captains over his thousands and captains over his fifties, will set some to plow his ground and reap his harvest, and some to make his weapons of war and equipment for his chariots. He will take your daughters to be perfumers, cooks, and bakers. And he will take the best of your fields, your vineyards, and your olive groves, and give them to his servants. He will take a tenth of your grain and your vintage, and give it to his officers and servants. And he will take your male servants, your female servants, your finest young men, and your donkeys, and put them to his work. He will take a tenth of your sheep. And you will be his servants. (1 Sam. 8:11–17)

Then he said, "And you will cry out in that day because of your king whom you have chosen for yourselves, and the LORD will not hear you in that day" (1 Sam. 8:18). Knowing all this to be from the heart of God, they refused to hear Samuel, or God for whom he spoke.

Here is a tragic note to the life of Samuel: At a moment of crisis, his sons would not listen to him, the elders would not listen to him, and the people would not listen to him. Only God remained! One would have thought he would have given up, but he did not. He again turned to the Lord who had called him and led him, and remained His servant. If God was not going to abandon them, neither would Samuel, regardless of how it would affect the rest of his life. God was God, and He was in charge and He would do what was right and best, regardless of the sin of His people. How crucial this measure of trust in God is in the life of every believer!

Stop and examine your personal walk with God, or the walk of your family or your church. Are you *insisting* on any matter in your life that could be against the clear will of God in His Word? Have you already noticed that God did indeed grant you your request, but you have never been the same since? If God granted a selfish request, then intimacy with God is not there; neither is the blessing of God. It seems as if He has withdrawn His presence from you, and you can sense the difference in your life. Then be careful to study what God and Samuel do next in the life of God's people.

SAMUEL: USED OF GOD TO CHOOSE THE KING

Since God was now going to guide His people to choose a king, He would do it in a way that would, or should, deeply affect both the new king and His people. Even in this selection of a king they all would know that they must still follow God as their King! Their hearts must never shift their trust from God to their king. God alone would be able to give them victories over their enemies. Their king would only be able to do what God enabled him to do. If their hearts turned away from God, they would again be defeated, just like before, and their enemies would rule over them.

Again God spoke to Samuel "in his ear" even before he met Saul. God shared with Samuel all He wanted him to do in this process of choosing a king. God would make known to Saul that Samuel was His servant, that God had chosen him, and that God was going to make provisions for him to serve Him and His people faithfully.

It is important to notice that God uses ordinary events to make His will known. All this is recorded for us in 1 Samuel chapters 9 and 10. Saul and his servants are sent by his father to find their lost donkeys. Saul obeyed his father to go, but he could not find the donkeys. So he remembered that there was a "man of God" nearby (Samuel). Surely a man of God could tell them where the donkeys were. When Saul found Samuel, he discovered Samuel was also called a "seer" and a "prophet" (1 Sam. 9:9), and that he not only knew about the donkeys but all about Saul as well. This was Saul's first encounter with God's servant, and it left a lasting impression on him, as God intended. To be king of God's people, Saul needed to know God, and Samuel was really the only one who could bring this about. In Samuel, Saul had, from the very beginning of his leadership as king, a very trustworthy servant of God, and a true friend. Saul would have to ignore this relationship with Samuel to sin against God.

One of the most significant things God told Samuel to do was to tell Saul of God's provision of the Holy Spirit in his life. God would be with him and on him, and would guide him in all matters of being a king, under God as King. Samuel told Saul in great detail all that would come into his life. Samuel said to Saul:

> The donkeys which you went to look for have been found. And now your father has ceased caring about the donkeys and is worrying about you, saying, "What shall I do about my son?"
>
> Then you shall go on forward from there and come to the terebinth tree of Tabor. There three men going up to God at Bethel will meet you, one carrying three young goats, another carrying three loaves of bread, and another carrying a skin of wine. And they will greet you and give you two loaves of bread, which you shall receive from their hands. After that you shall come to the hill of God where the Philistine garrison is. And it will happen, when you have come there to the city, that you will meet a group of prophets coming down from the high place with a stringed instrument, a tambourine, a flute, and a harp before them; and they will be prophesy-

ing. Then the Spirit of the L ORD will come upon you, and you will prophesy with them and be turned into another man. And let it be, when these
signs come to you, that you do as the occasion demands; for God is with
you. You shall go down before me to Gilgal; and surely I will come down
to you to offer burnt offerings and make sacrifices of peace offerings. Seven
days you shall wait, till I come to you and show you what you should do.
(1 Sam. 10:2–8)

Then the Scripture adds, "So it was, when he had turned his back to go from
Samuel, that God gave him another heart; and all those signs came to pass
that day. When they came there to the hill, there was a group of prophets
to meet him; then the Spirit of God came upon him, and he prophesied
among them" (1 Sam. 10:9–10).

God never assigns anyone a significant task, especially as it affects His
people, but that he makes full and adequate provision of His presence with
them, on them, and in them, to complete His work as God has assigned it.
Once that provision has been made, there is no excuse acceptable to God
as to why it is not done His way. Not only this, but God let the people know
that Saul was now a different man, as God was preparing them to receive
His choice for their king. So Saul returned to his father, but did not tell his
father that Samuel had told him that he would be king.

You might be thinking, *But how does all this apply to me? I have not been
selected by God to be a king among His people*. It is vital to remember that you
are not merely looking at a historical event, you are seeing God revealing
Himself and His ways to His people who had just sinned in asking for a king,
and rejecting Him as their King. Here is where you will need to meditate
about your relationship with God, and His response to you, your church, or
your family. Further, if God has proceeded to select you for an important
assignment among His people, He will thoroughly equip you with His Spirit
to do it, and you will be fully accountable to obey Him, and let Him do His
will through you.

All three of the churches I pastored were in very bad spiritual condition as I assumed God's assignment to guide them into God's will for them. To me, in each situation it seemed impossible! But God had promised His Spirit would rest on me with wisdom, understanding, counsel, might, knowledge, and the fear of the Lord (see Isa. 11:2). I was to trust and obey Him, for He would guide His people through my leadership until they were doing His will, in spite of their past sins. This is indeed what I experienced in each of the three churches. Each said later that they experienced their best years ever while we walked together with God. But like Samuel, with God's people it would take constant teaching and guiding in the Word of God to obey His Word faithfully, as God instructed me week by week. Without the teaching and obedience there would have been no changes.

Samuel obeyed God and set Saul before the people. He reminded them of their sin in choosing a king, and rejecting God as their King (see 1 Sam. 10:19). Then the Scripture says, "So all the people shouted and said, 'Long live the king!' Then Samuel explained to the people the behavior of royalty, and wrote it in a book and laid it up before the LORD" (1 Sam. 10:24–25).

Here again it is helpful to meditate and make some decisions in your own life, as I have done all through this study. Did you notice what Samuel did as he obeyed all that God had told him to do? He kept a spiritual journal and laid it up before the Lord. It was a covenant, a vow before God, to remind himself, and the people of this solemn moment, that it was done *before God, and as unto God!* This would be a perpetual reminder lest they sin against this solemn moment and again bring the anger of God upon them for their disobedience. Do you keep a spiritual journal and record sacred moments that you spend before the Lord? Do you record, for yourself as a witness before God, the specifics of your conversations with God and the pledges you made to Him? This can become a carefully chosen deterrent to sin in the future and prevent you from losing the blessing and pleasure of God in your life or in the lives of your family or your church.

When God's people disobeyed God (and this time it was extremely serious with God), He assured them of His presence and gave them the strict guidelines for their life with Him in the future. The relationship was set, and the continued blessing of God in His covenant with them was reestablished. Now follows just how they would obey, and Samuel would be in their midst as God's servant and prophet.

A DEFINING MOMENT FOR GOD'S PEOPLE: THEY SEE SAUL AND MAKE HIM THEIR KING

It was inevitable that sooner or later the enemy would come out against the people of God. The enemy of God's people is relentless and ruthless, and any attempt at compromising or bargaining with him will lead to permanent impairment. Nahash the Ammonite came, and his condition for a covenant with Israel, even for them to serve him, was that he would put out the right eye of every person "and bring reproach on all Israel" (1 Sam. 11:2). You can never negotiate with the enemy and come away unaffected. The result of bargaining with the world will leave you scarred and crippled. Sin brings death to the souls of men and servitude to the enemy of the souls of men. When the children of God heard the enemy's terms, "all the people lifted up their voices and wept" (1 Sam. 11:4). Sin always wants total domination with great shame before a watching world, so as to bring reproach upon God's name. All sin is like this, with no exception. There is no lesser sin! Paul urges, "Abstain from every form of evil" (1 Thess. 5:22).

Now comes a *defining moment* for Israel, and for Saul, their new king whom they wanted to lead them out into battle against their enemies. "Now there was Saul . . . ," and he asked, "What troubles the people, that they weep?" (1 Sam. 11:5). Saul cared and asked the right question. When God's people are weeping, someone needs to have real personal care as to why they weep. Never merely get used to the weeping in the lives of God's people. Too many churches are full of weeping people because of difficulty in their marriages, their homes, or traumas that have come upon them suddenly, unexpectedly, and with great pain and fear. We have to ask, "Where are the Sauls [leaders] who are inquiring about the sound of weeping among God's people?"

Then comes a wonderful word: "Then the Spirit of God came upon Saul when he heard this news, and his anger was greatly aroused" (1 Sam.11:6). God had given Saul an assignment and a call. Not only that, but God had provided His Holy Spirit for Saul's life. This is how the promise of God manifested itself in Saul: His anger was greatly aroused. He began immediately to unite God's people to have one heart and one mind against the enemy and trust in God to deliver them. This he did, and the Spirit created a heart response in the people: "And the fear of the LORD fell on the people, and they came out with one consent [or as one man]" (1 Sam. 11:7). Is this not always the work of the Holy Spirit? The early church was:

1. of one heart and one soul (Acts 4:32);

2. unified in the Spirit (Eph.4:3); and

3. full of Godly fear (Acts 2:43).

This should always be the expectation from the people of God when the Spirit "comes upon them." Oh, that God's people today would walk in the fear of the Lord, with one heart and soul, and experience the unity that only the Spirit can create. Then the enemies of God's people will experience defeat at the hand of God on behalf of His people. The enemy was defeated (see 1 Sam. 11:11), and Saul immediately acknowledged, "Today the LORD has accomplished salvation in Israel" (v. 13).

With the enemy defeated by the hand of the Lord, led by their new king, Saul, Samuel urged all the people to gather at Gilgal, "and renew the kingdom there" (v. 14). Then Samuel led them to do several significant things:

1. They made Saul king;

2. they made sacrifices of peace offerings before the Lord;

3. and all the men of Israel rejoiced greatly (v. 15).

This, therefore, was a profound moment in the mind of Samuel and the people. This was a moment of restoration as they again came to God in fellowship as assured to them by God. This was indeed a *defining moment* for Israel, and for Samuel. They were "renewing the kingdom" once again. You could say that this was a moment of "spiritual revival" for the people of God.

In some ways this is the symbol of the Lord's Supper: reconciliation and peace with God through the sacrifice of His own Son and our Savior. God declares us not guilty by virtue of the death of His Son and our confident trust in Him and His salvation.

It affirms the kingdom of God and our unity together under God's covenant rule in our lives. Each Lord's Supper becomes a special *defining moment* for the people of God.

SAMUEL'S ADDRESS AT SAUL'S CORONATION

"Blameless!" This was Samuel's appeal to the people of God at the close of his ministry, and the beginning of Saul as their king. He gave a testimony, and a solemn witness before Saul, the people, and before God. Saul needed to clearly know the secret of Samuel's ministry before the people of God. This would of necessity be what must characterize Saul as king too. The people also needed to know that living a life above suspicion was God's requirement for every leader of His people. This is God's requirement for every pastor and every leader (see 1 Tim. 3:2; Titus 1:6). This does not mean *sinless*, but it does mean *blameless*—no one can find any fault. Samuel asked the people specifically if they could find any fault in the way in which he walked among them, and they answered, "'You have not cheated us or oppressed us, nor have you taken anything from any man's hand.' Then he said to them, 'The LORD is witness against you, and His anointed is witness this day, that you have not found anything in my hand.' And they answered, 'He is witness'" (1 Sam. 12:4–5).

Jesus said it this way in the Beatitudes: "Blessed are the pure in heart, for they shall see God" (Matt. 5:8). The writer of Hebrews affirmed this by saying that God disciplines His people for "holiness . . . without which no one will see the Lord" (Heb. 12:10, 14).

Samuel affirmed that he was blameless, and he did it "before the LORD" (1 Sam. 12:3), and announced to God's people, "The LORD is witness" (v. 5). This was a *defining moment* for Samuel. God had said to His people that He would raise up for Himself "a faithful priest who shall do according to what was in [His] heart and in [His] mind" (1 Sam. 2:35). Samuel was now in his old age affirming what God had said. This can be a solemn and *defining moment* for each of us. At this time in my own life, God has called me before Him to give an account of how I have faithfully walked with Him. It is a very solemn moment for me, and God is not through with me. A Christian must not wait until the close of his life to take a spiritual inventory before God. Then, sadly, it may be too late! Do it regularly, and do it with transparent honesty—before God!

Too many of God's chosen leaders are not finishing well. Before God's people, and before God, they are not concluding the call of God with the word *blameless*. They may be forgiven, but they are not *blameless*. Again, I did not say without sin. I said that their behavior before the people of God in their calling is *blameless*—that is, there is no charge laid against them in their shepherding of God's people.

Samuel now did what every church must do corporately (gathered together to hear). Reciting the mighty deeds of God for His people, and how the people of God responded to His goodness, was seen as absolutely necessary for Samuel. He carefully challenged the people about their integrity before God, saying, "Stand still, that I may reason with you before the LORD concerning all the righteous acts of the LORD which He did to you and your fathers" (1 Sam. 12:7). Then, beginning with Jacob, through Moses and the judges, down to their present moment, he spoke of the faithfulness of God and the faithlessness of God's people—their fathers. He recounted the cycle of their walk with God: (1) God blessed them; (2) they forsook Him and followed after other gods; (3) God put them into bondage; (4) they cried out to God for His deliverance after a time; and (5) He heard their cry and sent deliverers, even Samuel himself.

He reminded them now, in the presence of God as their witness, that when they saw an enemy, they said to Him, "'No, but a king shall reign over us,' when the LORD [their] God was [their] king" (1 Sam. 12:12). How many times have God's people trusted in human leadership, human wisdom, and human vision—when God had been for them Wisdom, Vision, and Leadership? Leaders (elders, deacons, or other leaders) stood firm *in their own desires and wisdom*, and refused to listen to the people who warned that "without faith it is impossible to please [God]" (Heb. 11:6). Those who would walk by faith and trust in God, those who had been leading them faithfully over the years, even quoting from their founding fathers how they trusted God and how He did mighty works among them, were overruled by the loud and influential voices of a few. How tragic! How fatal! God will not allow, even today, His people to touch His glory. He will not allow His people to turn from trusting Him to any other gods, which is so common in our day. He still wants to display Himself to our world—through His people.

What may be some of the gods or the worldly influences around us that are offensive to God, and for which He will judge His people? First, a god is *anything* God's covenant people turn to for help when God told them specifically they were to turn to Him. There are no substitutes for Him. And we literally deny His glory when we turn to something, or someone else, instead of Him. Read carefully David's instruction from the Lord in Psalm 50:15: "Call upon Me in the day of trouble; I will deliver you, and you shall glorify Me."

Every time we turn to God by deliberate choice, He steps into the life of His people and delivers them (provides, sustains, gives victory)—and He receives glory before a watching world. The world sees *Him,* and often stands in awe and wonder at His power, or provision, or intervention, or goodness! Not to call on Him denies Him the glory that is rightfully His. He has eternally chosen to display Himself through His people who trust in Him and therefore call on Him. What are some of the things of the world (culture) around us to which we too often turn? One example is the banks, or other lending institutions, when we need finances, instead of leading God's people to trust in God and His Word and His promises—

> My God shall supply all your need according to His riches in glory by Christ Jesus. (Phil. 4:19)

or

> God is able to make all grace abound toward you, that you, always having all sufficiency in all things, may have an abundance for every good work. (2 Cor. 9:8)

or

> His divine power has given to us all things that pertain to life and godliness, through the knowledge of Him who called us by glory and virtue, by which have been given to us exceedingly great and precious promises, that through these you may be partakers of the divine nature, having escaped the corruption [depravity] that is in the world through lust. (2 Peter 1:3–4)

There are countless promises of God to which His people can, and should, turn, so that when we do, God acts powerfully and great glory comes to Him. His people will be encouraged and blessed, and a watching world will be drawn to Him.

Jesus also made this abundantly clear when He told His disciples, "Whatever you ask in My name, that I will do, that the Father may be glorified in the Son" (John 14:13). He went on to stress this turning to Him by adding, "If you ask anything in My name, I will do it" (John 14:14).

But God's people too often turn to the world, not only for finances, but for:

- marketing ideas, from such places as Disney World, Broadway, or the corporate world—instead of believing what He said in John 6:44, 45, 65: "No one can come to Me unless the Father who sent Me draws him . . . 'And they shall all be taught by God.' Therefore everyone who has heard and learned from the Father comes to Me . . . Therefore I have said to you that no one can come to Me unless it has been granted to him by My Father."

- one-on-one counseling—instead of the body (the local church) bringing the healing to the members.

- help in establishing "our vision," when God said that His people are not guided by *their vision*, but by His revelation (see Prov. 29:18).

- leadership principles, applying those of the world instead of the spiritual leadership commanded in the Scriptures.[1]

Samuel then commanded them, at God's instruction, that even though they now had the king they requested, their trust and hope must remain firmly with God. The king himself must also fully trust and depend on God. They were still a covenant people of God, and His covenant with them was still fully in place. Samuel declared to them:

- "If you fear the LORD,
- and serve Him

- and obey His voice,

- and do not rebel against the commandment of the LORD,

- then both you and the king who reigns over you will continue following the LORD your God" (1 Sam. 12:14).

Then comes the necessary other part of the covenant with God: "However, if you do not obey the voice of the LORD, but rebel against the commandment of the LORD, then the hand of the LORD will be against you, as it was against your fathers" (1 Sam. 12:15).

As God so often did, to convince His people to follow Him and obey Him, He demonstrated His incredible presence and power among them. How much must God do to convince His people that He is God, and they are not? When will God's people learn to *be* the covenant people of God, and live by His truths? What must God do to convince them not to rebel or forsake Him? This moment was another *defining moment* for Samuel, and for the people of God. God led Samuel, before the people, to call on Him in prayer to send thunder and rain "that day [in the harvest season]." God did, in a God-sized way, and "all the people greatly feared the LORD and Samuel" (1 Sam. 12:18).

> **How much must God do to convince His people that He is God, and they are not?**

God had done this with His people at the very moment of the initial covenant at Mount Sinai. His purpose, Moses declared, was "that His fear may be before you, so that you may not sin" (Ex. 20:20). When God's people lose the *fear* of God, they also lose the fear of *sin*. And when they lose the fear of sin, they are of no use to God. When they are no longer usable by God, He disciplines them for the purpose of restoration or, as the Scripture states, "For if you return to the LORD, your brethren and your children will be treated with compassion by those who lead them captive, so that they may come back to this land; for the LORD your God is gracious and merciful, and will not turn His face from you if you return to Him" (2 Chron. 30:9).

There is no question that the people of God in our day have indeed lost the fear of God, and also the fear of sin. They really do not believe that God will judge their sin. "He is a loving God," they say, "and He will not judge us. He forgives us when we ask Him to do so, and blesses us." We have literally "shaped God in our own image" (what we want Him to be for us), and are far from the God who has revealed Himself in Scripture. But the tragedy is that God *is* the same, and He does deal with His children as the covenant in Scripture reveals. He warned the church at Ephesus of impending judgment if they did not return to their first love (see Rev. 2:1–7). God always takes sin seriously!

DEFINING MOMENT: SAMUEL'S ROLE

The dynamics of God's love for His people when they sin grievously against Him are incredible, and give encouragement to us also, for the potential of revival, when we are at our lowest spiritually. From the presence of God, and therefore the heart of God, Samuel assures the people, "Do not fear . . . the LORD will not forsake His people, for His great name's sake, because it has pleased the LORD to make you His people" (1 Sam. 12:20, 22). God's people must never forget the great heart of God for His people:

- The LORD will not forsake His people;

- for His great name's sake;

- because it has pleased the LORD to make you His people.

Let's look at each of these a bit closer. *First,* "The Lord will not forsake His people"! Once God chooses to make a covenant with a people, He keeps His word. Hear His Word from Deuteronomy 31:6: "Be strong and of good courage, do not fear nor be afraid of them; for the LORD your God, He is the One who goes with you. He will not leave you nor forsake you" (see also Josh. 1:5; Heb. 13:5). This truth runs all the way through the Bible from the heart of God toward His people.

Second, His faithfulness is because "of His great name's sake." God's *name* was His character. It was what He would be known by. He had revealed His name through His mighty deeds, including creation. When God did a mighty work, His people gave Him a name that described God to them by their new experience with Him.

His name did something special for His people. God knew the world around them would be watching Him. He wanted them to know His nature so they would also respond to Him. So here Samuel said that God's kindness to them, in spite of their sin, was because of His great name—which He would reveal by what He did for them. The greater the need for His mercy, the greater is His name to His people.

Third, Samuel said God's response to them was because "it pleased the LORD to make you His people." That choice did not lie in them, but in God. He simply chose to "set His love upon them." Read carefully a fuller statement of this as recorded by Moses in Deuteronomy 7:6–11, and discuss this with others, especially as it relates to each of us today:

> For you are a holy people to the LORD your God; the LORD your God has chosen you to be a people for Himself, a special treasure above all the peoples on the face of the earth. The LORD did not set His love on you nor choose you because you were more in number than any other people, for you were the least of all peoples; but because the LORD loves you, and because He would keep the oath which He swore to your fathers, the LORD has brought you out with a mighty hand, and redeemed you from the house of bondage, from the hand of Pharaoh king of Egypt. Therefore know that the LORD your God, He is God, the faithful God who keeps covenant and mercy for a thousand generations with those

who love Him and keep His commandments; and He repays those who hate Him to their face, to destroy them. He will not be slack with him who hates Him; He will repay him to his face. Therefore you shall keep the commandment, the statutes, and the judgments which I command you today, to observe them.

God chooses—because He loves! Remember how Jesus made this very clear even to His disciples, when He reminded them, "You did not choose Me, but I chose you and appointed you that you should go and bear fruit, and that your fruit should remain, that whatever you ask the Father in My name He may give you" (John 15:16).

It pleases God to make us (you) His people! No merit in us, no gifts or talents in us, no status and influence in us determines God's choice to make us His children. It is always purely His love! This is why God wants a love response back from each of us, and why Jesus' question to Peter after his great failure was, "Do you love Me?" This is always His question to each of us. This very moment He waits for our answer, and He is looking at our hearts, and the life that is now proceeding from our hearts.

NINE

PRAY AND TEACH

For I know the thoughts that I think toward you, says the LORD,
thoughts of peace and not of evil, to give you a future and a hope.
Then you will call upon Me and go and pray to Me,
and I will listen to you

Jeremiah 29:11–12

WHEN GOD'S PEOPLE REBEL AGAINST YOU AND GOD, only time alone with Him can bring your life into line with the heart and purposes of God! This is what Samuel had to do, and the result was incredible. Before God, and His people, Samuel declared what he had settled with God: "Moreover, as for me, far be it from me that I should sin against the LORD in ceasing to pray for you; but I will teach you the good and the right way" (1 Sam. 12:23).

There is no question that this was a *defining moment* for Samuel. It was in the presence of God that Samuel knew his role at this time in his life. His role was typical of all spiritual leaders: (1) Never cease to pray for God's people, convinced that to fail to pray would be a sin against God; and (2) teach! Teach what is the good and right way. This is what the apostles did: prayed and taught the people of God. A people who are prayed for and taught "to observe [practice] all things that [Christ has] commanded" (Matt. 28:20) will be a people used of God to change an entire world. The church in the early chapters of Acts was just such a church. Ordinary people, taught daily by the apostles, "went everywhere preaching the word" (Acts 8:4). Later, the Bible states, "the churches throughout all Judea, Galilee, and Samaria . . . were multiplied" (Acts 9:31).

The very life of the people of God would rest on the prayer life and the teaching of God's servant Samuel. So significant was Samuel's prayer life that each time God's people got into great trouble, they cried to Samuel to pray for them (see 1 Sam. 7:8; 12:19). This is not only a *defining* moment for Samuel, but a *revealing* moment for him. This moment dramatically revealed his heart for God. He did indeed come to know and do what was in the mind and heart of God. This is what God looked for and raised up for Himself (see 1 Sam. 2:35). Little did Samuel realize how his intercession would save the people of God from the anger and wrath of God.

This is a good moment to recall several other persons God "raised up for Himself" for such times as these, as well as a time when He looked for someone like this but did not find one, so He destroyed the land.

LEADERS RAISED UP FOR GOD

First is Abraham, as God moved against the godless cities of Sodom and Gomorrah, in Genesis 18:16–19:29. God was looking for someone who would stand before Him for the land and know what was on His heart. God reasoned within Himself whether to let Abraham know what He was about to do (see Gen. 18:17). Then God made known the one to whom He revealed His heart:

> And the LORD said, "Shall I hide from Abraham what I am doing, since Abraham shall surely become a great and mighty nation, and all the nations of the earth shall be blessed in him? For I have known him [that is, become intimately acquainted with him], in order that he may command his children and his household after him, that they keep the

way of the LORD, to do righteousness and justice, that the LORD may bring to Abraham what He has spoken to him." (Gen. 18:17–19)

Then comes one of the most intimate conversations between Abraham and God, as God reveals to him what is on His heart, and Abraham pleads with God about the cities—because some of his family reside there. Though God did not spare the cities, for the sin was too great, He did save Abraham's nephew and his family: "When God destroyed the cities of the plain, . . . God remembered Abraham, and sent Lot out of the midst of the overthrow, when He overthrew the cities in which Lot had dwelt" (Gen. 19:29).

Then there was Moses, on top of Mount Sinai, pleading with God for His people. God had announced that He would slay them all because of their sin (see Ex. 32:8–10). Then began an intercession of Moses before the Lord: "Then Moses pleaded with the LORD his God . . . So the LORD relented from the harm which He said He would do to His people" (Ex. 32:11, 14; see Deut. 9:18–20, 25–29; 10:10–11).

Now God was looking for someone else to represent His people, and this was Samuel. Would he also never fail to pray for them, before God? To fail to pray, as a God-chosen servant of God, would be to sin against God. This Samuel was determined not to do, regardless of how His people sinned or how they would respond to him and his leadership.

The apostle Paul also was constantly reminding God's people in the churches of how he prayed unceasingly for them (see Rom. 1:9; Eph. 1:16; Phil. 1:3–4; Col. 1:3). It is so evident, especially to Paul, that the life of the people of God in the churches, and God's great eternal purpose through them, rested, first of all on Paul's praying for them, and then teaching them! And of course, these two essentials are seen and expressed preeminently in the life of Jesus with His disciples. The global purposes of God for the rest of the world rest on these two elements: (1) praying for the people of God; and (2) teaching the people "to practice" all that God has commanded them in His covenant relationship with them.

In praying for them, God revealed His heart for them. This caused the one praying to rise up and obey the Lord with His people. In teaching them, He could place on their hearts and minds all that God had commanded them in their lives before Him as His people. The blessing of the rest of the world waits on both of these.

I served as a pastor for about thirty years. It was a formidable task, for I literally was an "ambassador for Christ" among them, and it was "as though God were pleading through [me]: . . . be [and remain] reconciled to God" (2 Cor. 5:20). Throughout these special years in my life, I was consciously aware of this calling of God, and its implications. I, too, felt that I would sin against God if I either failed to pray for them or failed to teach them "the right and the good way" of God. I fearfully believed what Jesus taught God's people, that there was a very "narrow . . . gate and difficult . . . way which leads to life, and there are few who find it" (Matt. 7:14). They had to have someone to lead them and to teach them and to pray for them. God mandated through the Scriptures for every leader of His people to be this way. To pray and teach is also commanded by God for every father (and mother) concerning their children, for God's purposes to be worked out in them. And it certainly is true for every denominational and ministry leader of God's people.

Just as it was a *defining moment* for Samuel, it is right now a *defining moment* for each of us as well! I constantly am asking several important questions of myself in the midst of God's call and claim on my life for His people:

- Am I taking God's call on my life for His people seriously at this moment?

- Am I in serious prayer for them constantly?

- Do I see lack of prayer and intercession as sin against God?

- Can I say honestly that I am teaching all of God's people to practice everything that Christ commanded?

- Am I teaching them the "right and good ways" of God—the difference between the holy and unholy, and the clean and the unclean, as God commanded—especially in this culture when the world has been shaping and affecting the values of God's people?

God eternally purposed that through His people "all the families of the earth shall be blessed" (Gen. 12:3; Acts 3:25). As God's people are prayed for and taught by their leaders, the gospel will be preached to all nations and all peoples in the entire world. If they are neither prayed for fervently nor taught to live out all God has commanded, the rest of the world will suffer spiritually, and eternally. God forbid that this should ever be so, since we know God's Word for the leaders of His people!

There are yet six important truths that Samuel shared with God's people during this *defining moment* in his life and ministry: (1) Fear the Lord; (2) serve Him; (3) in truth; (4) with all your heart; (5) for consider what great things He has done for you; (6) if you do wickedly, you shall be swept away, both you and your king. These are merely another way to describe God's covenant with His people, the positive and the negative. All are always present when God covenants with His people individually or corporately!

FEAR THE LORD

First, God begins with "Fear the LORD your God." Hear Moses, who guided God's people into their first covenant: "And now, Israel, what does the LORD your God require of you, but to *fear* the LORD your God?" (Deut. 10:12, emphasis added). This is constant throughout God's relationship with His people. We have briefly shared this previously, but here it is crucial—again. A healthy fear of God is essential to God's people retaining a fear of sin and keeping clean and holy their significant and unique relationship with God.

SERVE HIM

Second, they were to serve Him. They, as His servants, were to "deny self, take up their cross, and follow Him" (see Matt. 16:24) as their Master and Lord. They were not to serve any other gods found in the culture around them. They were literally to seek first (as priority #1) His kingdom (rule) and His righteousness—and all else would be added to them (see Matt. 6:33). They were to diligently seek Him and His will with all their hearts, souls, minds, and strength—and serve Him. They were to *do* everything He commanded them to do—at all times, under all circumstances and conditions—and at every command. They were His servants, and they were therefore to *serve* Him. This was a crucial condition of the covenant—and it remains to this day. Would you stop and consider carefully if your conduct would position you clearly as a "servant" of God? What commands are you implementing through your life? How earnestly are you seeking to know His will so you may do it immediately and diligently? And your church? Are you seeking sincerely to know His will and do it completely and immediately? These are not idle questions; they are at the heart of our relationship with God. This is why Samuel included this as essential to Israel's immediate relationship with God.

What commands are you implementing through your life?

TRUTH

Third, the people of God were to serve Him "in truth." That is, they were never to take to themselves a defining of God's will for their lives. They were always to go back to the Scriptures (Law), read it carefully, and follow it faithfully. The truth had already been given and stated clearly. They were to know it and do it to the letter, leaving nothing out. There were no nonessentials in the covenant with God. They were to serve God "in truth."

If the people of God ever got away from or failed to know thoroughly the truth of God, they would sin against God.

Moses, in Deuteronomy 32:46–47, stated clearly, "Set your hearts on all the words which I testify among you today, which you shall command your children to be careful to observe—all the words of this law. For it is not a futile [vain] thing for you, because it is your life." He had previously stated, "Know that man shall not live by bread alone; but man lives by *every word* that proceeds from the mouth of the LORD" (Deut. 8:3, emphasis added).

In the New Testament Jesus said, "I am the way, the truth, and the life. No one comes to the Father except through Me" (John 14:6). He also said clearly, to a large crowd and to His disciples, "It is the Spirit who gives life; the flesh profits nothing. The words that I speak to you are spirit, and they are life" (John 6:63). This is why Jesus, at the close of His ministry and just before He returned to the Father, urged His disciples; "teaching them [the new believers] to observe all things that [He] commanded [them]" (Matt. 28:20). And as the Father did with His people in the Old Testament, He assured them, "Lo, I am with you always, even to the end of the age." For the covenant people of God, *every word from the mouth of God is their very life.* This was true with Jesus as well, and therefore is crucially true for every believer today.

So the truth of God must be taught faithfully to God's people, by those instructed by God to teach. When the people are not taught, they depart from the Word of God, and self-destruct. They fall into their own ways, and sin against God and experience the loss of the life of God.

I remember, following an evening worship service where I had spoken, a well-dressed lady came to me requesting that I pray for her. I assured her I would be happy to pray with her. I asked her what it was that she wanted me to pray about. She replied, "I am going to my lawyer tomorrow morning to seek a divorce from my husband. Would you pray with me about this?" I asked if her husband was a Christian, and she assured me that he was. I then replied, "I will be happy to pray with you. But you need to know what I will be praying!" I turned to Malachi 2:16, "For the LORD God of Israel says that He hates divorce, for it covers one's garment with violence."

She looked at me in shock! She said, "I have been to three Christian counselors, and each of them has encouraged me to divorce my husband. Why did no one ever show me this Scripture?" I told her I did not know, but this is the heart of God toward His children: God hates divorce! She sobbed for some time, then asked me again: "Will you pray for me? I am going to my lawyer and ask him to cancel my divorce proceedings, and I am going to seriously seek reconciliation with my husband!" I did pray with her, and earnestly pleaded with God to save her marriage, as a witness to His mercy, grace, and love. To fail to follow and live by God's Word is fatal to one's life. How do you measure the pain and loss in a divorced marriage—including the pain in each life and the lives of the children—for years? And what about the sorrow in the lives of parents and grandparents—even in the life of their church family? When God said, "The wages of sin is death, but the gift of God is eternal life" (Rom. 6:23), He was warning His people of the seriousness of sin (not obeying His Word). I have been a pastor for more than thirty years, and in ministry for more than forty-five years, and no one can convince me that there is no "spiritual destruction" in divorce! God hates divorce! We must realize as believers that it is important that we live by the fact that *every* word is from the mouth of God! But God's people, in the Scriptures and to this day, must be taught the ways and Word of God.

In the same book of Malachi, God indicted the priests for not teaching the people. As a result, the people were straying from God and experiencing the consequences of their sin. The leaders were at fault for the people's sin:

> "And now, O priests, this commandment is for you.
> If you will not hear,
> And if you will not take it to heart,
> To give glory to My name,"

Says the LORD of hosts,

"I will send a curse upon you,

And I will curse your blessings.

Yes, I have cursed them already,

Because you do not take it to heart . . .

Then you shall know that I have sent this commandment to you,

That My covenant with Levi may continue,"

Says the LORD of hosts.

"My covenant was with him, one of life and peace,

And I gave them to him that he might fear Me;

So he feared Me

And was reverent before My name.

The law of truth was in his mouth,

And injustice was not found on his lips.

He walked with Me in peace and equity,

And turned many away from iniquity.

For the lips of a priest should keep knowledge,

And people should seek the law from his mouth;

For he is the messenger of the LORD of hosts.

But you have departed from the way;

You have caused many to stumble at the law.

You have corrupted the covenant of Levi,"

Says the LORD of hosts. (Mal. 2:1–2, 4–8)

Jesus was just as thorough concerning God's Word. He assured His disciples, "If you abide in My word, you are My disciples indeed. And you shall know the truth, and the truth shall make you free . . . Therefore if the Son makes you free, you shall be free indeed" (John 8:31–32, 36).

All parents must ask themselves, "Are we diligently teaching our children not only what the Word of God says, but teaching them to practice all the Word of God in their lives?" Even more important than that, are the spiritual leaders of God's people faithfully teaching all the people of God the Word and ways of God, and leading them carefully to practice the Word of God in their lives? If we do not teach the people of God, then we are leaving the people to sin against God, following their own thoughts and ways and not the ways of God. This is fatal to God's people, and to the community and nation in which they live.

For the leaders to return to God and ask Him to lead them into all the Word of God which He knows His people have neglected, ignored, or discarded, is absolutely essential. Then to ask the Holy Spirit to guide them and His people to know again and practice His Word—this will bring about a great revival in the land. Returning to a faithful observance of the Scriptures is always present in great revivals and awakenings. The truth of God sets people free!

WITH ALL YOUR HEART

Fourth, God's people were to do this "with all their heart"! Partial obedience is, to God, disobedience! A divided heart is an abomination to God, for a divided heart has permitted a "rival" to God's right to be God in their lives. By creation, no one can serve two masters. To allow anything else to rival the pure and total love of God in the heart is to place other gods there. We will turn to them instead of Him. But He alone is our Life. There are no substitutes for God. Without Him, we "can do nothing" (John 15:5).

Further, the very *essence* of God's covenant with His people is found in this command: "Hear, O Israel: The LORD our God, the LORD is one! You shall love the LORD your God with all your heart, with all your soul, and with all your strength. And these words which I command you today shall be in your heart" (Deut. 6:4–6).

It is amazing that these very words, called today the Shemma, are quoted and recited every day by the Jewish people as a mandatory religious practice. It is the very essence of their covenant relationship with their

God—and ours too! It would do us well, also, if we repeated these words from our heart at the beginning of every day and throughout the day, as a constant reminder of our covenant with God!

God was always looking at the *hearts* of His people: "The LORD looks at the heart" (1 Sam. 16:7; see 1 Kings 8:39; 1 Chron. 28:9; Jer. 17:10; Acts 1:24). It was always the heart that shifted from God first, then the life moved away from the ways of God and the relationship with Him. God was always warning His people about guarding their hearts, for He knew that "out of it spring the issues of life" (Prov. 4:23). He constantly warned, "But if your heart turns away so that you do not hear, and are drawn away, and worship other gods and serve them, I announce to you today that you shall surely perish" (Deut. 30:17–18). The slightest shift in the heart away from God can be fatal and devastating. When God does not have one's heart, He knows, sooner or later, He will not have anything else.

Jesus asked Peter one very important question because He knew how easily Peter's heart could shift: "Simon, son of Jonah, do you love Me more than these?" (John 21:15). Three times this question confronted Peter, and three times Peter painfully answered, "Yes, LORD, You know that I love You!" Jesus knew that if He had Peter's heart, He had everything else too! This has always been true, from Genesis through the entire Bible. This is the one question He would ask of each of us. And God reads the heart, not merely the lips. As a matter of fact, Jesus once said to the people who kept saying they believed in Him, *"These people draw near to Me with their mouth, and honor Me with their lips, but their heart is far from Me"* (Matt. 15:8; quoted from Isa. 29:13).

One of the clearest pictures of why God wants total response from the heart is seen in Jeremiah 29:11–14:

> For I know the thoughts that I think toward you, says the LORD, thoughts of peace and not of evil, to give you a future and a hope. Then you will call upon Me and go and pray to Me, and I will listen to you. And you

will seek Me and find Me, when you search for Me with all your heart. I will be found by you, says the LORD, and I will bring you back from your captivity; I will gather you from all the nations and from all the places where I have driven you, says the LORD.

The *whole heart* is the only response and relationship that is acceptable to God. Anything less will rob us of God's best!

> **The *whole heart* is the only response and relationship that is acceptable to God.**

Under Samuel's leadership, the sinning people of God were once again commanded to "serve Him in truth with all [their] heart[s]" (1 Sam. 12:24). Nothing else would do. This was the essence of their covenant with God. This alone would keep them in a relationship of love with God, and would bring all the covenant blessings of God. This was a *defining moment* for Israel. They knew the Law (though it seems obvious that the leaders had not been teaching them faithfully). They had the record of God dealing with their fathers. They had the immediate experience of total disaster with the Philistines and the ark of God, and now they had again the clear instruction from Samuel, their respected spiritual leader and prophet. What they did next would reveal their hearts toward God, and would ultimately determine the future, for them and their children. We know what happened next. They did not heed the voice of God and therefore experienced the anger and judgment of God, just as He said they would. We will look at this later.

YOUR DEFINING MOMENT!

Stop right now, in your own reading and study, and let God examine your heart. He knows your heart, regardless of what *you* think or say. I know that you would want to be certain of *God's* clear evaluation of your heart. It is your life, and therefore, your future. Ask the Holy Spirit to show you, from God's Word, His guidelines for your life and behavior. Let the Holy Spirit convict you of sin and righteousness. Know His love is sure and perfect and that He wants the best for your life. He is persistent in His love, and will not leave you to live in sin and therefore miss His eternal purpose for you. It is always wise and good to take a spiritual inventory of your heart on a regular basis. If you do not, your heart may stray from God without your being aware of it. The discipline of God will then take place and it will be too late for you to prevent His action against your sin. You have His Word. You have His Holy Spirit, your Teacher. You have all you need to keep your heart tender and focused before God. You have the promises of God that He wants to bless you, and He will. What a *defining moment* this can be for you!

CONSIDER GOD'S MIGHTY DEEDS

Fifth, Samuel instructed God's people: "Consider what great things He has done for you" (1 Sam. 12:24). There is nothing stronger than this command. God knew that if His people were to consider and meditate on His mighty deeds that were done on their behalf, they would love, trust, and follow Him. His mighty deeds expressed His love for them. His actions on their behalf revealed His faithfulness to His covenant with them. God not only spoke, but He acted on what He spoke. When He spoke, He did it. Isaiah knew this well, as he said:

> The LORD of hosts has sworn, saying,
> "Surely, as I have thought, so it shall come to pass,
> And as I have purposed, so it shall stand . . .
> For the LORD of hosts has purposed,
> And who will annul it?
> His hand is stretched out,
> And who will turn it back?" (Isa. 14:24, 27)

159

There was never a moment that God ever purposed in loving His people that He did not do it. The record stood. They could recall His mighty acts on their behalf. He not only spoke of His love for them, but He actually loved them! And now they were being commanded by God to bring all His mighty deeds to remembrance. God could say, "Stand before Me, and remember! Have I ever failed you? Have I ever forsaken you? Have I ever failed to do one thing that I promised to you? Why, then, have you been forsaking Me?" With all the evidence in front of them, God would be vindicated, and they would be found guilty.

We, who are the people of the "new covenant," stand even more guilty when we do not keep His commands. Paul felt this, as he reminded the believers:

> If God is for us, who can be against us? He who did not spare His own Son, but delivered Him up for us all, how shall He not with Him also freely give us all things? Who shall bring a charge against God's elect? It is God who justifies. Who is he who condemns? It is Christ who died, and furthermore is also risen, who is even at the right hand of God, who also makes intercession for us. Who shall separate us from the love of Christ? Shall tribulation, or distress, or persecution, or famine, or nakedness, or peril, or sword? As it is written:
>
> > "For Your sake we are killed all day long;
> > We are accounted as sheep for the slaughter."
>
> Yet in all these things we are more than conquerors through Him who loved us. For I am persuaded that neither death nor life, nor angels nor principalities nor powers, nor things present nor things to come, nor height nor depth, nor any other created thing, shall be able to separate us from the love of God which is in Christ Jesus our Lord. (Rom. 8:31–39)

God can clearly say also to us, "What more could have been done to My vineyard [to you] that I have not done in it?" (Isa. 5:4). He can, and does, command us to stand before Him and give an account of how we have been walking faithfully in His ways. And He will ask us to stand, observe, and recall what He has done for us in the Cross, the Resurrection, and Christ's ascension. What more could He have done for us? Recall all His mighty deeds, and put them alongside our responses to Him, and stand accountable before Him.

He has been doing this in my life recently! He has been reminding me of the power of the Cross, the Resurrection, and Pentecost. He has been reminding me what it cost Him to make a way into "the Holiest by the blood of Jesus . . . consecrated for us, through the veil, that is, His flesh" (Heb. 10:19–20). Then He is asking me (and He does have this right in His covenant with me), "What more could I have done for you, to provide My power through your life? I have a right to expect 'fruit' in you—much fruit! But I am not finding the kind and measure of the fruit that I had a right to expect!"

I stand guilty before Him. I have been crying out, as David did,

> Have mercy upon me, O God,
> According to Your lovingkindness;
> According to the multitude of Your tender mercies,
> Blot out my transgressions.
> Wash me thoroughly from my iniquity,
> And cleanse me from my sin.
>
> For I acknowledge my transgressions,
> And my sin is always before me.
> Against You, You only, have I sinned,
> And done this evil in Your sight—
> That You may be found just when You speak,
> And blameless when You judge.

161

Behold, I was brought forth in iniquity,

And in sin my mother conceived me.

Behold, You desire truth in the inward parts,

And in the hidden part You will make me to know wisdom.

Purge me with hyssop, and I shall be clean;

Wash me, and I shall be whiter than snow.

Make me hear joy and gladness,

That the bones You have broken may rejoice.

Hide Your face from my sins,

And blot out all my iniquities.

Create in me a clean heart, O God,

And renew a steadfast spirit within me. (Ps. 51:1–10)

Take time, right now, to recall all the mighty deeds God has done for you.

Take time, right now, to recall all the mighty deeds God has done for you. Look at what He has done for you in the Scriptures. Then recall all the goodness of the Lord in your life that He has done in His faithfulness to you. Remember your heritage, His protection in moments of crisis or temptation, His provision and His watchcare over you, your marriage, and your children. Recall the marriage partner He prepared for you and brought to you. Ponder His call on your life, and His great salvation given so freely to you. Meditate on the mercy He has shown you when you did not deserve it, and His grace to you. Oh, His grace to you! List them all, and see if your life matches in gratitude and fruit what God has been expecting to find.

JUDGMENT

Sixth, Samuel faithfully reminded them of the other side to the covenant they had made with God: "But if you still do wickedly, you shall be swept away, both you and your king" (1 Sam. 12:25). The people of God *must* hear this side of the covenant! They must see all the activity of God, since the time in which God made His covenant with His people (pictured first in Exodus 19–20, and spelled out in detail through the rest of Exodus and Leviticus). A summary of this relationship was clearly given in Deuteronomy 28. You may want to stop and review this chapter carefully. You may also want to review Matthew 5–7 (Sermon on the Mount), Matthew 10, and Romans 5–8. This vital relationship and accountability is seen also in the living Christ's words to the seven churches of Asia Minor in Revelation 3–4 (read Revelation 1–5 to catch the fuller picture from God's perspective).

There was no way God's people could ever misunderstand their relationship with their God. He had done all He could to make it plain. They must now guard their hearts, listen to instruction, and do all He commanded. It was their very life! The thunder had come and the fear of God was present. The way of God was stated one more time. What more could God have done for them? And God, in mercy, had granted to them a king, as they had requested. The king, Saul, had been present during all this renewal of God's people. Now it was time for Saul to live out before God and the people his rule as king, under the King. The life of the people of God would depend on Saul's faithfulness. The spiritual leaders always hold the key to the lives of God's people. How did Samuel, God's servant and prophet, live out his relationship with God in the midst of His people? He prayed for them and taught them: "Moreover, as for me, far be it from me that I should sin against the LORD in ceasing to pray for you; but I will teach you the good and the right way" (1 Sam. 12:23).

Regardless of what fellow Christians are doing, regardless of what is happening in Washington, regardless of what church leaders do, as for me, far be it from me that I should sin against God by ceasing to pray for you! Do not forget, not only would Samuel pray for them but he would teach them the good and right way. That is an astounding *defining moment* for what a prophet does when the people of God sin against God. What would you do? Lambaste them?

I talked with a group from a seminary recently. They asked me: "What are the common people of God saying about the seminaries?"

I said, "Let me tell you one experience. I spoke with a dear lady who was very hesitant to ask a question."

She said, "I really don't want you to think I am being smart; I am not. I am serious about this question. Do the seminaries have a course that teaches the pastors how to lay a guilt trip on the people?"

Everything within me turned upside down.

She said, "Every pastor who does not get his way starts to leave a guilt trip on the people to make them feel that they are the problem."

But what about Samuel? Did he blame them? What does a prophet do when he is serving the people and they do not do what he believes God wants them to do? He said, "Moreover, as for me, far be it from me that I should sin against the LORD in ceasing to pray for you; but I will teach you the good and the right way" (1 Sam. 12:23).

The Lord could ask us a simple statement, "Did you die for them?" Remember 1 John 3:16? We should lay down our lives for our brother. Now could I ask you to take a spiritual inventory of your prayer life and concern for the most rebellious in your church? Are you praying *for* them or *at* them?

Would you be like James and John on the road to Samaria when they asked, "Lord, do You want us to call down fire and burn them all up?" Can you imagine others, as they walked across Samaria and saw this lump of coal, asking, "What brought these charcoals?" The answer could be, "Well, two of God's servants were rejected when they wanted others to do something for them, so they prayed down fire from heaven."

Jesus' answer would be, "I didn't come to destroy but to save." In the book of Acts the Spirit of God told Philip to go down to Samaria, because from the day that Jesus led the Samaritan woman to the Lord and the whole city of Sycar was redeemed, the Father was continuing to take the gospel to the surrounding towns. The next town was Samaria. And God sent Philip down to see what He had been doing. Revival broke out. They had to send Peter and John. And the Bible says they experienced one of the greatest revivals all over Samaria. They went back to Jerusalem preaching in all the cities of Samaria. I think Jesus may have said, "If I did what you had asked Me to do, there would have just been ruins."

Jesus had a different kind of fire He wanted to bring. We might want to bring a fire that destroys, but Jesus would bring a fire that redeems and brings revival. I could say to you that in those moments when your church reaches a low point and you want to ask God to bring fire and destroy, that is the time and place when God could bring His greatest revival.

> Then Samuel said to the people, "Do not fear. You have done all this wickedness; yet do not turn aside from following the LORD, but serve the LORD with all your heart. And do not turn aside; for then you would go after empty things which cannot profit or deliver, for they are nothing. For the LORD will not forsake His people, for His great name's sake, because it has pleased the LORD to make you His people. Moreover, as for me, far be it from me that I should sin against the LORD in ceasing to pray for you; but I will teach you the good and the right way. Only fear the LORD, and serve Him in truth with all your heart; for consider what great things He has done for you. But if you still do wickedly, you shall be swept away, both you and your king." (1 Sam. 12:20–25)

Can you see the quality of the message? What does the prophet do in this moment when the people had sinned, chosen a king, and God had given them what they requested? He keeps on proclaiming God's good news to the people of God and warning them of disastrous things if they do not return to Him.

TEN

OBEDIENCE IS BETTER THAN SACRIFICE

Behold, to obey is better than sacrifice,
And to heed than the fat of rams.

1 Samuel 15:22

THERE ARE NO SUBSTITUTES FOR OBEDIENCE. Hard work, being director of the prayer ministry, serving as a deacon, teaching Sunday school, leading a home Bible study, or being on church visitation are no substitutes for obedience. This definitive statement requires meditation. The prophet speaks at a moment when the king they had chosen had completely disobeyed God. The king said he was obeying when he was living in disobedience. Do you know anyone who insists he is obeying right in the middle of his disobedience? Partial obedience is disobedience. There is no such thing as partial obedience. Call it what God calls it—rebellion and disobedience! How serious is disobedience in the mind of God? He calls it rebellion. Not only does He call it rebellion, but He defines *rebellion* as "the sin of witchcraft, and stubbornness is as iniquity and idolatry." Then He said to Saul, through Samuel, "Because you have rejected the word of the LORD, He also has rejected you from being king" (1 Sam. 15:23).

> **How serious is disobedience in the mind of God?**

"I am just a stubborn old mule," some people say. How does God look on stubbornness? Be careful that you do not take a personality test and then live out your stubbornness because the test said that this is the way you are! This Scripture says, "Stubbornness is as iniquity and idolatry." Do not treat lightly your stubbornness as though it is an inherited quality you have to live with. The Scripture says that when God saves you, you become a new creation—the old is gone. Everything has become new. God's goal is to conform you to the image of His Son. God did not give His only Son to die on a cross and be raised from the dead so He could bless your personality traits. He gave His Holy Spirit to make a change in your life. Whatever you used to be, God is trying to conform you to the image of His Son.

The right question to ask is, "What kind of personality did Jesus have?" God is trying to make you like His Son, regardless of what the world is trying to tell you. You need to tell the world that God told you what kind of person you are to be. If you ask God, He will tell you He is trying to conform you to the image of His Son. I am a long way from what I am going to be, but I am a long way from where I used to be. God just keeps on working on us.

This is a strange instant in the life of Samuel when he tells Saul the Lord has rejected him from being King. For in some ways he seems to go into obscurity from this moment. And then there is a very common but sad moment a few chapters later. The Bible simply states, "And Samuel died. And they buried him." When I read that, having gone through his precious life, I wept. I thought, *Is that all they will say about this precious servant of God?*

> Then Samuel died; and the Israelites gathered together and lamented for him, and buried him at his home in Ramah. And David arose and went down to the Wilderness of Paran. (1 Sam. 25:1)

There came a pain over my heart when I read that. Is that all they say about God's servant? Then the Lord reminded me what John the Baptist said in

John 3: "He must increase, but I must decrease" (v. 30). There is a point when the only one left standing on the field is God. Not you, not your reputation, nothing, just Him. But this moment in Samuel's life when he related the rejection of the King seemed to be quite defining. It was the moment when he had to announce that Saul had been rejected and his reign was over. His kingdom had been taken from him and was now given to another.

SAMUEL AND THE NEW KING

"Saul reigned one year; and when he had reigned two years over Israel . . ." (1 Sam. 13:1).

It seems to be going well—but an ominous feeling is developing about what is now taking place in Saul's heart. His heart is the key to his reign as king. God had said this in the beginning; now it would be evident if his heart remained true to God, and therefore to his people.

Then, the enemy came against them! Two things will always test your heart: (1) the passing of time, and (2) when the enemy comes against you. In both of these you really cannot play catch-up in your relationship with God, and it is here that everything else is determined.

"Then the Philistines gathered together to fight with Israel, thirty thousand chariots and six thousand horsemen, and people as the sand which is on the seashore in multitude. And they came up and encamped" (1 Sam. 13:5). It is now evident that the people no longer trusted in the God who had done mighty things for their fathers and had promised to do so for them. For it now reads, "when the men of Israel saw that they were in danger . . ." (1 Sam 13:6). Circumstances were changing, but with God as their God, were they really in danger? Of course not! But if you do *not* keep a daily intimacy with God, and obey what He is saying each day, you will surely be overcome by circumstances when a crisis looms before you. This is what happened, "When the men of Israel saw that they were in danger (for the people were distressed), then the people hid in caves, in thickets, in rocks, in holes, and in pits" (1 Sam. 13:6). What a pitiful sight. The people of God, who were serving the God of the universe, were now cowering before mere men. No matter what the circumstances looked like, they should never have responded like this!

As you read on in this moment-of-truth for Israel, human reasoning may lead you to be in great sympathy with the people and with Saul. But you must see this moment, and similar moments in your own life, *from God's perspective*! At this moment Saul responded with partial obedience—but partial obedience is disobedience, and disobedience is unacceptable with God and denies His people of His victories. Saul did wait seven days, "according to the time set by Samuel" (1 Sam. 13:8). This was right. But there was more to the ways of God than that. Only Samuel could offer the required sacrifice before they went into battle. They had to wait not only the seven days Samuel suggested, but until Samuel came, according to God's instruction. The directives of men cannot, and must not, overrule the commands of God. Saul acted now on human reasoning: The enemy was near, the people were scattering, and Samuel had not yet come. Was it not logical for the king to offer the sacrifice for the people? For did they not have to immediately enter into battle with the enemy? After all, he was the king and the people would follow him, and he would then lead God's people into battle.

But this would be clear disobedience to God's command! Logical reasoning never cancels the commands of God! Urgency does not cancel God's Word. The urgency and the immediate apparent danger should have led to the strictest obedience. Their lives depended on it. How true is the Scripture, "There is a way that seems right to a man, but its end is the way of death" (Prov. 14:12).

Then came a *defining moment* for Saul: (1) It revealed the condition of his heart toward God, and (2) it cost him his kingdom! The passage simply states, "Now it happened, as soon as he [Saul] had finished presenting the burnt offering, that Samuel came." When the heart is wrong, the one who sins not only expects his work to be accepted, but to be praised. So Saul "went out to meet him [Samuel], that he might greet [bless] him." But Samuel said, "What have you done?" (1 Sam. 13:10–11). I do not know the tone in Samuel's voice, but I believe it was a combination of fear [of God], and sorrow and anger at Saul. For now Samuel knew what God would do next! No amount of reasoning and excuse would atone for Saul's sin against God. He had disobeyed, thus revealing his heart, and would learn the serious nature of obedience and disobedience, even to only one of God's commands. One act of disobedience makes you a disobedient person! And this may make you unacceptable to God, especially to lead His people. All the logic and the reasoning of Saul as to why he offered the sacrifice instead of waiting on Samuel left *one* thing out—obedience to God!

Samuel's response to Saul's sin of disobedience is a classic answer to sin, by a prophet of God.

> And Samuel said to Saul, "You have done foolishly. You have not kept the commandment of the LORD your God, which He commanded you. For now the LORD would have established your kingdom over Israel forever. But now your kingdom shall not continue. The LORD has sought for Himself a man after His own heart, and the LORD has commanded him to be commander over His people, because you have not kept what the LORD commanded you." (1 Sam. 13:13–14)

A moment of disobedience to any one of God's commands is a *defining moment*! It defines what God will do next in a person's life. Disobedience reveals the condition of the heart. Having a heart of obedience is always God's requirement for any servant of His. The king, Saul, was to remain a "servant of God" and not merely a servant of the people. Many leaders of God's people forget this and simply do what the people want or what they think best for their people. But God is looking for "those whose heart is loyal to Him" (2 Chron. 16:9). It became painfully clear that Saul's heart was not loyal to God. This made him unacceptable to lead God's people. The people must hear clearly from God. Only a leader whose heart is loyal to Him can do this! Remember, they are a covenant people of God. They are not merely ordinary people like the nations around them. They were a "special treasure" to God (Ex. 19:5). They had not chosen God; He had chosen them—for Himself (see Ex. 19:6).

Disobedience reveals the condition of the heart.

This is what Jesus said also to His disciples: "You did not choose Me, but I chose you and appointed you that you should go and bear fruit, and that your fruit should remain, that whatever you ask the Father in My name He may give you" (John 15:16). Paul also knew this when he said to the Ephesian believers, "For we are His workmanship, created in Christ Jesus for good works, which God prepared beforehand that we should walk in them" (Eph. 2:10). Thus, obedience to everything Christ commanded, and God revealed to them as His will, was vital to God. It also determined their relationship with God. God is very serious about His eternal purposes being worked out through His people! Besides, His people are to live out their relationship with Him before a watching world. The unbelieving world would get their clearest understanding of God by what they saw of His activity in and through His people. If His people were not obedient, it would affect what the world would see and know of God Himself!

Saul would soon know that he was not indispensable! God had someone else in mind who would have a heart like His, and would obey Him. He could, and would, be replaced by another person. In this exchange, the Spirit that was upon Saul to do his work as king would be withdrawn from him. When the assignment is no longer there, the Spirit is no longer needed to enable him. The Spirit would now come upon David, who was called of God to take Saul's place (see 1 Sam. 16:13–14). This important truth will be discussed and applied in detail later in this book. It is interesting to note at this point, however, that the evidence that God's Spirit was not available to Saul's whims is seen in 1 Samuel 14:37. Saul inquired of the Lord as to whether he should go down against an enemy. This was important to an assured victory. Is this the will of God or not? But the Scripture reveals this altered relationship with God in Saul's life: "So Saul asked counsel of God . . . but He did not answer him that day."

Saul's heart continued in disobedience, and once again Samuel, God's servant, was involved. Once again God was about to deal with the evil king, Amalek, for what he had done earlier to Israel. So God, through Samuel, came to announce this to king Saul (the entire account is found in 1 Sam. 15). Samuel once again reminded Saul of the absolute necessity of obedience to God: "Samuel also said to Saul, 'The LORD sent me to anoint you king over His people, over Israel. Now therefore, heed the voice of the words of the LORD'" (1 Sam. 15:1). Obedience was a command by God to Saul. Samuel was the prophet assigned to deliver this message. Because of this, Samuel's heart would know, understand, and grieve over any disobedience. The one closest to the heart of God always has a much bigger picture than anyone else. This is often why the Scripture speaks of "the burden which the prophet . . . saw" (Hab. 1:1).

The command of God to Saul was, "Now go and attack Amalek, and utterly destroy all that they have, and do not spare them" (1 Sam. 15:3). The record is clear concerning the disobedient heart of king Saul: "But Saul and the people spared Agag and the best of the sheep, the oxen, the fatlings, the lambs, and all that was good, and were unwilling to utterly destroy them. But everything despised and worthless, that they utterly destroyed" (1 Sam. 15:9).

Then came some chilling words from God to Samuel. The effect of God's Word to him was devastating! "Now the word of the LORD came to Samuel, saying, 'I greatly regret that I have set up Saul as king, for he has turned back from following Me, and has not performed My commandments.' And it grieved Samuel, and he cried out to the LORD all night" (1 Sam. 15:10–11). The king may not have realized that God was aware of all he had done, but God made Samuel aware, and Samuel cried to the Lord all night long!

Several truths stand out at this moment. The sin of a leader is shared and practiced by the people he leads. It states, "Saul *and the people.*" God knew this would happen. As goes the leader, so go God's people. He could not allow this to continue much longer, so He confronted Saul one more time. This time the disobedient heart of Saul was not only revealed by his answers to Samuel, but his fate was securely sealed. This was a most painful moment for Samuel. The sin of the king was multiplying and affecting God's people again. As Samuel went to meet the king, he was told that Saul had gone to "set up a monument for himself" (1 Sam. 15:12). When Samuel finally caught up with Saul, the hardness of his heart came out immediately, as his greeting to Samuel was, "Blessed are you of the LORD! I have per-formed the commandment of the LORD" (1 Sam. 15:13). This conversation between Saul and Samuel is incredible. The deceitfulness of the heart, in the presence of the knowledge of God, is enormous in its implication and outcome.

> **As goes the leader, so go God's people.**

Samuel merely asked, "What then is this bleating of the sheep in my ears, and the lowing of the oxen which I hear?" (1 Sam. 15:14). Saul's explana-tion is close to blasphemy! In effect he said, "My dis-obedience is here to offer to God as a sacrifice!"

This was one of the most painful of the *defining moments* for Samuel. His closeness to God made the sin of Saul most griev-ous. The closer to God, the more sinful is sin. The holiness of God creates an awareness of the grievous nature of sin! Holy indignation overcame Samuel, and he said to Saul, "Be quiet!" (v. 16). Then he added, "I will tell you what the LORD said to me last night." Then Samuel revealed to Saul what God had said: "When you were little in your own eyes, were you not head of the tribes of Israel? And did not the LORD anoint you king over Israel? Now the LORD sent you on a mission, and said, 'Go, and utterly destroy the sinners, the Amalekites, and fight against them until they are consumed.' Why then did you not obey the voice of the LORD? Why did you swoop down on the spoil, and do evil in the sight of the LORD?" (1 Sam. 15:17–19).

There are several important and crucial truths about God seen in this word from Samuel to Saul:

1. Any word from God is an absolute! It cannot, and must not, be violated by man.

2. God sees all we do (i.e., "in His sight"). Nothing is hidden from the Lord once He has given us a command.

3. No variation in God's commands is permitted, no matter how logical or reasonable it may seem to us.

4. There is always a radical accountability: "God is not mocked; for whatever a man sows, that he will also reap" (Gal. 6:7).

5. When God responds to our disobedience, it is severe and thorough and final.

6. Disobedience to God's command is considered as "evil in the sight of the Lord." Samuel knew all this, and experienced incredible pain. He knew God!

Samuel watched, with horror, a hardened heart sinning against God. Saul said: "But I have obeyed the voice of the LORD, and gone on the mission on which the LORD sent me, and brought back Agag king of Amalek; I have utterly destroyed the Amalekites" (1 Sam. 15:20). Then Saul did what so many do: He blamed the people, and even attributed good motives to their disobedience. They spared the best, "to sacrifice to the LORD your God in Gilgal" (1 Sam. 15:21). Notice the change in Saul's relationship to God when he said, "to the LORD *your* God." No longer *his* God, or *the people's* God, but *Samuel's* God! How tragic! Before the final curtain comes down on Saul and his relationship to God, I need to help us apply this moment to our lives.

Reading this *defining moment* in Saul's life can leave us careless toward our own lives, in our relationships with God. I have known many individuals who have been confronted by God to "go on His mission" either at home or somewhere in the world. God had an enormous purpose in His heart for this assignment. They responded, and went. Then, in the midst of their assignment, circumstances seemed to change. They immediately began to make excuses, used human reasoning, and abandoned their obedience to God's call. They forsook their assignment and returned home, leaving the assignment unfulfilled. Many have found that their relationships with God were never the same again. However, their reasoning and explanations for disobedience remain, even to this day. And to the observer of their lives, the Spirit for their assignments has been removed, and God has assigned someone else to those same assignments. The Lord is not mocked. When He gives an assignment He expects absolute obedience. Nothing short of this is acceptable! No substitutes will do! When God gives a command, there is too much at stake. His commands are not suggestions! They are commands that are to be obeyed fully.

This spirit of disobedience can run through a church, or a family. I have noticed that when parents disobey God with a hardened heart and seemingly have no conscience about it, their children also feel free to ignore or disobey God in their lives. When a family sees their children in disobedience, as a pastor, I encourage them to look carefully, in the presence of God, to see if they may be living in disobedience in some area of their own walks with God. As go the parents, so often go their children.

Someone may seek God about carrying some position or responsibility in their church. They proceed, and then circumstances or people change, and they resign, sometimes in anger or deep frustration. However, they seem to be indifferent to their disobedience to God. But to God, their obedience remains a serious matter, and reveals their heart before Him. Any vow (commitment to obey) made to God is very serious. The writer of Ecclesiastes says, "When you make a vow to God, do not delay to pay it; for He has no pleasure in fools. Pay what you have vowed—better not to vow than to vow and not pay" (5:4–5).

Samuel then makes one of the most significant statements in his life about God, and how God looks on obeying Him:

> So Samuel said:
> "Has the LORD as great delight in burnt offerings and sacrifices,
> As in obeying the voice of the LORD?
> Behold, to obey is better than sacrifice,
> And to heed than the fat of rams.
> For rebellion is as the sin of witchcraft,
> And stubbornness is as iniquity and idolatry.
> Because you have rejected the word of the LORD,
> He also has rejected you from being king." (1 Sam. 15:22–23)

Let me spell out carefully the truths found in this brief but powerful statement:

1. Obeying the voice of God (His commands and directives) is far more significant than making an offering. Offerings are important, but not nearly as important to God as obeying Him.

2. Disobedience is sin.

3. Disobedience is rebellion against God.

4. Disobedience is seen by God as the sin of witchcraft.

5. Disobedience is seen as stubbornness.

6. Disobedience is, to God, iniquity and idolatry.

7. Disobedience is rejecting the word of God and therefore rejecting Him.

8. In rejecting Him, He rejects you.

Obedience to God is the key to life! It is the key to the kingdom of God (see Matt. 7:21–24). Obedience is like building your house (life) on a rock. It will not be shaken or moved when the storms of life come (see Luke 6:46–49).

Now comes one of the most difficult of truths faced in the Bible. Is there a line over which, if you pass, there is no return? The answer is, "Yes!" This is seen clearly here in the life of Saul, and Samuel is the one ordered by God to make it clear to Saul. In effect Samuel had to say to the king, "You have crossed over the line with God, and there is no return. Your kingdom has now been taken from you, and given to another. No amount of repentance can bring back the favor of God. It is over for you!"

Quick repentance, because he was caught, was unacceptable! Even though Saul cried out to Samuel, "I have sinned, for I have transgressed the commandment of the LORD and your words, because I feared the people and obeyed their voice. Now therefore, please pardon my sin, and return with me, that I may worship the LORD" (1 Sam. 15:24–25). It was *too late*! What awful words! No recovery with God! Saul's actions revealed the set of his heart. He repeatedly disobeyed God. Repentance for this particular disobedience did not change the set of his heart, and God knew that this was so. When God makes a judgment about the heart, His judgment is true. And when God passes judgment, it is so, and remains so. No amount of pleading with God will change it. This is the clear statement about Esau and his heart: " . . . profane person like Esau, who for one morsel of food sold his birthright. For you know that afterward, when he wanted to inherit the blessing, he was rejected, for he found no place for repentance, though he sought it diligently with tears" (Heb. 12:16–17). Too late!

I have witnessed many a servant of God who transgressed against God.

Only when caught or exposed did they eagerly repent. But their repentance was too late, and too little. It was not acceptable to God. He may have forgiven them, but they were never again restored to their former position of leadership. Their heart had been exposed as hardened in rebellion and sin against God over a long period of time. On their own they did not repent. Only when confronted by God, through another of His servants, did they acknowledge their sin. This was inadequate before God. They may even insist on being restored, and get very angry with God's people for not heeding them. I have heard them say, "If God can forgive me, why can't you?"

Sometimes I will respond by saying, "It is not a matter of God's forgiveness. It is a matter of *character*. God can instantly forgive, but it takes much longer to develop character." And character is the absolute prerequisite for leadership of God's people. If a person has lived in rebellion and sin over a prolonged period of time, it clearly indicates a character problem. Quick repentance when exposed is never adequate with God for a person to be restored to leadership. Saul had consistently failed to obey God. It was a character problem, and therefore he was eliminated from God's service. His consequent behavior revealed that God's judgment on his character was absolutely correct.

Here is a *defining moment* for each of us. Taking a spiritual inventory of our walk with God is vital. It will also define much of the rest of our lives with God. I have said many times that our lives are the products of choices we have made—with God! If you are now in sin or rebellion against God's commands in your life, decide quickly and thoroughly to repent—turning from your rebellion and disobedience and returning to a real covenant relationship with God. He does forgive. He does restore the heart to Himself. He will cleanse and heal any life that desires, from the heart, total obedience to God and His will for his or her life.

However, you may want to examine your walk with God, remembering His call on your life and any decision to disobey that call. You may want to see if God has removed His Spirit of enabling from your life if you are no longer serving in that call. If so, go before the Lord and ask for mercy. Return your life to Him, on His terms, in total gratitude for His kindness to you in any way. Release your life to Him and His perfect love for you, and accept *anything* He may entrust to you, no matter how small in your eyes. It is, for any of us, more than we deserve, and more than we can handle. I am grateful that He entrusts to me any opportunity to represent Him anywhere. The most remote or insignificant place of service is certainly more than I deserve. Only His great mercy grants and entrusts to me any place of service to Him.

Samuel now had to be very firm with Saul. Samuel was God's servant, not the king's. He was obligated to God, and not to the king and his desires. Samuel could not grant the king's request, for he would himself be disobedient to God, and this he would not do. So Samuel had to say to the king: "I will not return with you, for you have rejected the word of the LORD, and the LORD has rejected you from being king over Israel" (1 Sam. 15:26).

Saul did not want to take no for an answer. He was king and should be heard and followed. But he was not dealing with a man now, but rather with God! And it was too late! In desperation Saul grabbed hold of Samuel's robe and tore it. Samuel's response was one of a true prophet. He said, "The LORD has torn the kingdom of Israel from you today, and has given it to a neighbor of yours, who is better than you. And also the Strength of Israel will not lie nor relent. For He is not a man, that He should relent" (1 Sam. 15:28–29).

The king made one last, desperate plea to the prophet, who now was himself grieving for Saul: "I have sinned; yet honor me now, please, before the elders of my people and before Israel, and return with me, that I may worship the LORD your God" (1 Sam. 15:30). Once again, notice the heart of Saul toward God, as he says to Samuel, "your" God! What a moment for Samuel. He was not God, but His servant. He did return with Saul, and Saul worshiped the Lord.

But Samuel knew so much more about God than the king. So he was determined to obey what God had said, even if the king would not. Samuel ordered Agag, king of the Amalekites, brought before him, and he publicly killed the king. It says clearly that Samuel did this "before the LORD" (1 Sam. 15:33).

The issue of King Saul was settled with Samuel forever. The record indicates, "Samuel went no more to see Saul until the day of his death. Nevertheless Samuel mourned for Saul, and the LORD regretted that He had made Saul king over Israel" (1 Sam. 15:35).

There is an incredible pain in being a prophet of God. When the people you love and grow up with will not obey the God you serve, your intimate relationship with God takes precedence; but the pain of knowing what God will do next can be almost overwhelming. The pain for Saul just would not go away for Samuel. Suffering is a normal part of being a servant of God. Every believer who would serve God with all his or her heart will endure pain and suffering. The pain that is the most real and persistent will be the pain associated with the disobedience of God's people. Paul even said, "I bear in my body the marks of the Lord Jesus" (Gal. 6:17). Rather than withdrawing from his assignment from God, Samuel carried the pain for the rest of his life.

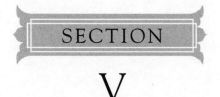

SECTION

V

ANOINTED BY GOD

*This will be the behavior of the king who will reign over you:
He will take your sons and appoint them for his own chariots
and to be his horsemen, and some will run before his chariots.
He will appoint captains over his thousands and captains over
his fifties, will set some to plow his ground and reap his harvest,
and some to make his weapons of war and equipment for his
chariots. He will take your daughters to be perfumers, cooks,
and bakers. And he will take the best of your fields,
your vineyards, and your olive groves, and give them to his servants. He will take a tenth of your grain and your vintage,
and give it to his officers and servants. And he will take your
male servants, your female servants, your finest young men,
and your donkeys, and put them to his work. He will take a
tenth of your sheep. And you will be his servants.*

1 SAMUEL 8:11–17

ELEVEN

GOD CHOOSES HIS KING

Then Samuel took the horn of oil and anointed him in the midst
of his brothers; and the Spirit of the LORD came upon David
from that day forward. So Samuel arose and went to Ramah.
But the Spirit of the LORD departed from Saul,
and a distressing spirit from the LORD
troubled him.

1 Samuel 16:13–14

AS WE LOOK AT THIS MOMENT IN SAMUEL'S LIFE when Samuel anointed David, we must keep in mind that Samuel is serving God in the midst of the people of God who had sinned against God. How do you behave when the people of God disobey Him? We need a word from God at this moment. God moves either in judgment or blessing. The behavior of the people of God does not stop the progress of the purpose of God or the kingdom of God. It means that those who could have been a part of God's purpose may be eliminated, and they may never know what could have been.

This is seen most dramatically when the leaders chose to encourage God's people not to trust Him to lead them into the promised land. In spite of all God had done for them to reveal His sovereignty and might, the elders believed both the circumstances they saw and the reasoning of their own hearts. God judged them severely and placed them all in the wilderness for

185

CHOSEN TO BE GOD'S PROPHET

forty years—until all these leaders had died. Those who rebelled died in the wilderness and never knew what could have been (see Num. 13:30–33; 14:26–32).

Have you ever thought about what could have been in Saul's life? Or what could have happened for the whole people of Israel if they had only obeyed? The tragedy was that when the king sinned, all of the people also chose to sin. When we stand before God and give account for the one life we each have to live, I believe the most severe moment of judgment will be when God briefly shows us what could have been if only we had obeyed Him. God may take you back to a time in your life when you refused to obey Him. Since that moment, years may have passed in your life. I think God is going to say, "Let Me take you back to the moment when I first spoke to you, and let Me tell you what could have been in those intervening years if you had not disobeyed Me." That should be a moment of meditating. May each of us say with one heart, "O Lord, may there never again come a time in my life when You give a command to which I say anything else but, 'Yes, Lord!'" Your relationship to God is revealed in how you spontaneously respond to God's commands. What should be your immediate and spontaneous response when God gives a command? Some people's problem is that they *do* know the will of God but have a rebellious heart and do not know if they want to follow or even know God's will. If you do not have a *spontaneous* "Yes, Lord," you need to go back and work through your relationship to the lordship of Jesus Christ. If every time God gives you a directive you wrestle with Him and argue with Him, you need to understand how strongly God responds to rebellion. God made a definitive statement to King Saul about disobedience to Him, within His covenant. Listen to how God responded to King Saul through Samuel:

> **Your relationship to God is revealed in how you spontaneously respond to God's commands.**

So Samuel said:

"Has the LORD as great delight in burnt offerings and sacrifices,

As in obeying the voice of the LORD?

Behold, to obey is better than sacrifice,

And to heed than the fat of rams.

For rebellion is as the sin of witchcraft,

And stubbornness is as iniquity and idolatry.

Because you have rejected the word of the LORD,

He also has rejected you from being king." (1 Sam. 15:22–23)

This came as a shock to King Saul. God said, in effect, "Saul, you just need to know who is on the throne! I am, and you are not. But in your rebellion and disobedience you are telling Me that you are, and I am not!" This audacity will not stand!

This Scripture now gives a picture of how God finally deals with Saul and how He chooses a man after His own heart. At this point, you need also to be aware that the Holy Spirit is very prominent in the Old Testament.

Then Samuel took the horn of oil and anointed him in the midst of his brothers; and the Spirit of the LORD came upon David from that day forward. So Samuel arose and went to Ramah. But the Spirit of the LORD departed from Saul, and a distressing spirit from the LORD troubled him. (1 Sam. 16:13–14)

God's Spirit always comes upon one when he is to lead God's people. This was true of Saul. He rebelled against the Spirit who was upon him as king. What does His Spirit do to the one He has rejected? He departs. I think God caused Saul never to forget his initial call, what could have been, what his sin was, and how much he had lost. It troubled him the rest of his life.

Did he immediately cease to be king? No. Saul continued to serve God's people as their king, but now he knew clearly that he was *rejected by God*. He continued as king for at least eleven or twelve more years. All this time Saul could have known and experienced the presence of God in the corporate life of His people. But God's Spirit was withdrawn from King Saul. He no longer had God's assignment, so he no longer had the enabling of God's Spirit to serve as king. Therefore, the Spirit given to him when he became king was no longer needed or available.

Whenever sin brings a canceling of God's call on a leader's life, the special anointing needed for fulfilling their assignment is withdrawn. He is no longer needed, for God has withdrawn His assignment. Does such a person often try to continue to function in his position? Yes, often, and sometimes for years like Saul. But his effectiveness never returns. The Spirit of enabling is withdrawn along with the assignment. I have often heard the plea of ministers who have gravely sinned against God say, "But I still sense God has called me, so I must be given an opportunity to serve!" I reply, "The reality of your call may, and often does, remain with you for the rest of your life. But God will not relent or return you to your specific call. You have sinned and are no longer blameless, which was God's requirement in your call" (see 1 Tim. 3:2, 10; Titus 1:6–7).

Sometimes those who feel such pain as Saul are missionaries who have sinned greatly, or just disobeyed God's original call and assignment. The Spirit of anointing needed in their calls is withdrawn, for they are no longer in their original calls. This same Spirit of enabling is now given to those who have replaced them in the fields where God had assigned them.

GOD'S TIMING

Many years passed from this anointing of David until he mounted the throne. In fact, it was eleven years. God's ways are not our ways. Especially is this true of God's *timing*! We are so certain, in our day, that the moment of God's calling *is* the timing! This may be true, but wait on God and let Him reveal His timing for your life.

Eleven years passed from the time of Joseph's dream (God revealing His assignment for him) to when he became next to Pharaoh. From Paul's call to his first missionary journey to the Gentiles was also about eleven years. And now, from the moment David was anointed king by Samuel at God's command until he became king over Israel was also about eleven years. When God anointed David, He did not say there would be smooth sailing right to the throne. For eleven years he was hounded all over the place. There was one point at which he had to pretend to be insane just to survive. Is this God's anointed one, upon whom the Holy Spirit dwelt? Yes. God's ways are not our ways.

Too often we are impatient doers. We feel we must immediately proceed the moment God speaks. This *may* be God's way for your life, and I would not neglect immediate obedience. But, if there are many obstacles that seem to be keeping you from what you know to be God's assignment, and God has not withdrawn His call—stay in the absolute mode of obedience *until* God's timing is revealed. Let me share with you what I sense God always does. There is a Scripture in the life of Jesus where Jesus displays mercy by saying, "Therefore be merciful, just as your Father also is merciful. Judge not, and you shall not be judged. Condemn not, and you shall not be condemned. Forgive, and you will be forgiven. Give, and it will be given to you: good measure, pressed down, shaken together, and running over will be put into your bosom. For with the same measure that you use, it will be measured back to you" (Luke 6:36–38).

Too often we are impatient doers.

In the ways of God, there is absolute correlation between how you treat your brother and how God treats you, regardless of how holy you proclaim yourself to be before God. I think God was saying to David at this time, "David, you do not know it yet, but there is coming a time in your life when you will need an extended measure of mercy. And even though I have rejected Saul, I want you to know I am a God of mercy. And My mercy extends over and over and I forgive seventy times seven (see Matt. 18:22)! I am going to let you and My people see the measure of My mercy to Saul. Because there will be a time when you will need Me to extend mercy to you. And you will remember that for eleven years I gave Saul an opportunity to repent until he drew his last breath. Then I let you be king." Later, when David killed Uriah and took his wife, Bathsheba, it was God's mercy that saved David's life. It was a mercy God taught him while He let Saul live as king for years after being rejected. The cry of David when he realized the seriousness of his sin was:

> Have mercy upon me, O God,
> According to Your lovingkindness;
> According to the multitude of Your tender mercies,
> Blot out my transgressions.
> Wash me thoroughly from my iniquity,
> And cleanse me from my sin. (Ps. 51:1–2)

God's answer, knowing David's repentant heart, was spoken by Nathan, who said "The LORD also has put away your sin; you shall not die. However, because by this deed you have given great occasion to the enemies of the LORD to blaspheme, the child also who is born to you shall surely die" (2 Sam. 12:13–14).

This truth needs desperately to be applied in our own lives. For instance, if God does not immediately grant you "your vision" for your ministry, do not be fussing with God. He may be extending mercy to someone else before He does something for you. Let this word of God be an absolute guide to your life as you walk with God.

I pastored a church where the treasurer often behaved in a terrible way toward anyone who asked a question about his report in our business meeting. Many began to pressure me to do something, or they would leave the church! I knew God, and His mercy, so I prayed with a pastor's heart. I lifted his life up before God. God was showing him mercy, and giving him time to change. It was not long before this man became ill and died within a week. I fell on my knees and wept before the Lord. I came to know something about the ways of God that I had never known by experience in my own life, and it continues to affect me to this very day. I learned this truth about God and seek to walk in the light of it.

Would that not be an important lesson to learn? Would you let God leave someone else in place, even though he is rejected of God, until God has extended His mercy to that one and furthermore continue to wait until God says, "Enough"? God will let you know when it is enough for your brother's sinful life. Don't try to bypass the timing of God or take matters into your own hands.

Don't try to bypass the timing of God.

It is important to see how a prophet shaped by God works in the midst of a people who sin. Samuel did not fail to bring discipline to God's people. But he let God show him how He wanted to do it. This is the way God preserved His people. Too often, when we take it upon ourselves to discipline the people of God, many are lost in the process.

Samuel saw the torch being passed. He knew God, and was being guided by the Holy Spirit. He knew how God had blessed Saul and how the Spirit had come upon him. Everything Saul needed to do the will of God was present when the Spirit of God came upon him. Samuel also saw how Saul behaved. Then he heard God say, "Samuel, let Me tell you how I am going to remedy this. Now I am rejecting Saul and am going to choose a man after My own heart. And when I find a man after My own heart and place My Spirit upon him, I want you to anoint him king. When I select a king, it will be settled." I think Samuel was coming toward the end of his life, and now he was well over eighty, maybe ninety, when he saw the Spirit of God come upon the young man David. God had announced to Samuel that this was the man who had a heart just like His. I think Samuel may have said then, "I think my work is done," for he slips into the background, and David comes to the place of prominence.

SAMUEL ANOINTS DAVID KING

Samuel, God's chosen servant, now had another significant assignment from God. He was to be directed by God to the leader God knew had a heart like His, and to whom He would now entrust His people. It was to be David, a young shepherd man. Psalm 78:70–72 indicates the heart of God, and His assignment for David's life:

> He also chose David His servant,
> And took him from the sheepfolds;
> From following the ewes that had young He brought him,
> To shepherd Jacob His people,
> And Israel His inheritance.
> So he shepherded them according to the integrity of his heart,
> And guided them by the skillfulness of his hands.

First Samuel 16 is full of the ways of God that must be carefully studied for our own lives today.

SAMUEL WALKS IN THE WAYS OF GOD

Samuel would lead the people according to the ways of God and not the ways of man! Later, God would carefully point out to His people through His prophet Isaiah:

> "For My thoughts are not your thoughts,
> Nor are your ways My ways," says the LORD.

"For as the heavens are higher than the earth,

So are My ways higher than your ways,

And My thoughts than your thoughts." (Isa. 55:8–9)

Samuel was learning that his thoughts were not always God's thoughts. He had so much more to learn about his relationship with God, and God's relationship with him and God's people. Samuel was in deep mourning for Saul. This is evident when the Scripture states, "Nevertheless Samuel mourned for Saul, and the LORD regretted that He had made Saul king over Israel" (1 Sam. 15:35). Samuel knew God and knew how God would deal with Saul's persistent sin and rebellion against God. The grief was real and deep in Samuel. Suffering and pain were not what Samuel expected as a part of the life of a servant of God, especially for a prophet! It is obvious, however, that Samuel felt that his sorrowing after Saul was appropriate and acceptable before God. Then God came to Samuel and showed him a side of His nature that was unknown to him: "Now the LORD said to Samuel, 'How long will you mourn for Saul, seeing I have rejected him from reigning over Israel? Fill your horn with oil, and go; I am sending you to Jesse the Bethlehemite. For I have provided Myself a king among his sons'" (1 Sam. 16:1).

A pure servant of God must keep his eyes and heart on his Master. He must not become sidetracked by circumstances, regardless of the level of pain involved. The Master determines the course of His servant's life. When the Lord made a decision about Saul, it was settled. After that decision God continued moving on in His eternal purposes, which created for His servant a new assignment. This new assignment would dramatically affect God's people—and Samuel. God's timing may not have been Samuel's, but it was God's. God asked how long Samuel was going to stay in the past. God had already rejected Saul and chosen another to take his place. Then God told Samuel that he was the one to bring this transition to pass.

To Samuel, something surely had to be different in the second choice of king over the first king. Saul, his friend, had been the one chosen and was a failure before God. What would God do differently now? Once again, God spoke directly to Samuel, saying: "Do not look at his appearance or at his physical stature, because I have refused him. For the LORD does not see as man sees; for man looks at the outward appearance, but the LORD looks at the heart" (1 Sam. 16:7).

GOD SPEAKS AND DIRECTS

It is extremely important at this point in our study to look carefully at a truth that runs throughout the life of Samuel. God spoke directly to him again and again, giving him immediate and clear instructions as to what he, His servant, must say and do as he walked among God's people. Since God's ways are not man's ways, God's perspective must always be sought, understood, and done. His perspective will always be very different from man's perspective. Therefore, God's servant must know Him and His ways, and be obedient to Him.

Let's look further into these truths, for they can dramatically affect our own walks with God as leaders among God's covenant people.

First, God always speaks to His servant, giving him / her God's heart and mind. Too many today do not believe that God still speaks to His people. Not only that, they do not believe that God gives *specific* directives. They feel man is left to figure out what is logical at the moment. They say that God left us only general spiritual guidelines, and that we must walk within these. But according to the Scripture, specifics *are* given to each of us.[1] This moment in Samuel's life graphically reveals how important the specific guidance of God is to any of His servants.

Second, God's ways are not man's ways. Israel's first king was chosen based on physical stature and appearance (see 1 Sam. 10:23–24), but in that choice he obviously did not have a heart that was conditioned toward God. Today, a pastor-search committee will often look at a man's educational credentials; then they will look at his age and physical appearance to see if he would make a good impression on their TV program for the church; they may look at the special qualities and attractiveness of his wife, and even his children. Man looks at the outward appearance. God does not even consider the outward appearance! God always measures a man by his *heart*. Character is more important to God than appearance. It is out of the heart that a man's life proceeds. If his heart is bad or inadequate, the life will be bad and ineffective. If the heart is good, the life will be good. The root system of the tree produces the fruit. The condition of the well produces the condition of the water that is drawn from it. God looks at the heart!

But only God can know the heart of a person. Therefore it is wise to seek the counsel of God in choosing a leader. To know that He has indeed guided you, as He promised to do, and did with Samuel, brings a great comfort and confidence and hope. The choice of a leader for God's people is so crucial to God that He will give very specific instructions in the choice. So you may ask about a person's walk with God or his patterns of intimacy with God. You may ask things such as when he arises to meet the Lord or about his time spent in God's Word. You might ask about his prayer life; listen to key phrases in his conversation, such as "God guided me" or "I sought the Lord," or "Our family takes all decisions before the Lord." Is there *any* evidence in his conversation that indicates clearly his intimacy of trust and reliance upon the Lord? To God, his walk with Him is the deciding factor—not merely the public impression he makes, the sound of his voice, or his pleasing personality. His heart is the real issue with God!

Third, God will reveal what He knows of the heart of a man. God revealed this to Samuel about David. The picture of this *defining moment* is seen in Acts 13:22–23: "And when He had removed him [Saul], He raised up for them David as king, to whom also He gave testimony and said, *'I have found David the son of Jesse, a man after My own heart,* who will do all My will.'"

Notice that God says the one who has a heart like God, "will do all My will." This Saul did *not* do, and therefore was of no use to God and His people. David was vastly different. He was not one who did not sin, but he was one who had a heart like God's and dealt with his sin as God directed him (see Ps. 51), doing it thoroughly and immediately. God revealed this to Samuel concerning David: "And the Lord said, 'Arise, anoint him; for this is the one!'" (1 Sam. 16:12). God's people are in a covenant relationship with God, so they must have a leader who not only walks with God, but knows clearly what the will of God is and does it.

Samuel's obedience was immediate—as it had always been from the time he was a little boy: "So Samuel did what the LORD said" (1 Sam. 16:4). From the beginning of Samuel's walk with God, not only did he obey God completely, but as he did, God affirmed to all the people that he was "established as a prophet of the LORD" (1 Sam. 3:20). So it was at this later moment in his life. He now had a track record before God and the people, and the Bible states, "The elders . . . trembled at his coming" (1 Sam. 16:4). Did they also know that they, too, had sinned against God in all that was transpiring in their midst, and were afraid Samuel had come to pass judgment on them? What an incredible reputation to have among God's people! I have to seriously ask, "If I am a servant of God, what do people say when I arrive in their midst? What is my track record with God in the eyes of God's people?" This is not a minor question; it is a serious one, and one that should be asked before God, for His name's sake.

Some very special people entered my life who had a deep impact on me. A retired missionary from China, Bertha Smith, had this effect. She had been through the great Shantung revival, and her life breathed the presence and the holiness of God. When she was present, there was a holy hush and a sense that everyone present needed to get ready for a radical encounter and accountability before God. She was fearless and extremely focused. God was always greatly feared and honored when she showed up. She was a very pleasant person—but always very serious about God and His people's relationship with Him. Samuel also had this effect on God's people.

GOD'S PROCESS OF SELECTING A KING FOR HIMSELF

The Scriptures are clear and very simple to read and understand, and therefore ought to be applied quickly and easily into our own lives and situations. But too often they are merely ignored. When we go to do the very ordinary things in the Christian life, we forget, or do not consult the Scriptures to be certain of God's ways. Notice the process:

- God gave a promise that He would guide in the selection of a new king.

- Samuel believed God, and proceeded obediently.

- The process began, and man's ways were immediately pressed on Samuel by the sons of Jesse. They did not even think of young David. He did not fit their profile.

- Samuel kept waiting on God until . . .

- God stepped in and announced to Samuel: "Arise, anoint him; for this is the one!" (1 Sam. 16:12).

- Samuel took the horn of oil and anointed him in the midst of his brothers.

- "And the Spirit of the LORD came upon David from that day forward" (1 Sam. 16:13).

- There was a sequel to all this that vindicated both God and Samuel in the eyes of all: "But the Spirit of the LORD departed from Saul, and a distressing Spirit from the LORD troubled him" (1 Sam. 16:14).

The *ways of God* seen in these few verses are clear and simple. God always works in simple and clear ways that a child could understand and follow. They are not always the same (they rarely are), but they are simple and clear for those seeking a word from God. Obedience is the key! It is not man's logic, reasoning, or thinking, but God's *revelation* that is important. This profound-yet-simple truth is stated clearly in the New Testament also:

> Where is the wise? Where is the scribe? Where is the disputer of this age? Has not God made foolish the wisdom of this world? For since, in the wisdom of God, the world through wisdom did not know God, it pleased God through the foolishness of the message preached to save those who believe. (1 Cor. 1:20–21)

Again, notice the activity of God! First, He gives an assignment. The assignment now is for David to be king over God's people. Second, those He assigns He thoroughly equips by placing His Spirit upon them. Third, if the assignment is rejected or disobeyed, He withdraws both His assignment and His Spirit. He may, and often does, give the assignment to another who has a heart like His, and places His Spirit upon him. When His Spirit is withdrawn from a person formerly chosen, a distressing spirit accompanies him, giving evidence to all that this one has been rejected by God. However, all too often this rejected one does not realize that the process is even taking place. I see it all the time. Unless someone leads him through the Scriptures, like this *defining moment*, he often remains angry and even bitter toward God. He may also blame the people, thinking those people are the reason he can no longer serve.

Somehow, spiritual leaders must learn several things about the nature of God and the ways of God. They are clearly revealed (not by human reasoning) by God in the Scriptures:

- God can, and will, reject a chosen leader, if God knows his heart has changed and the person no longer knows, listens to, or obeys His voice.

- One should never try to bypass the sovereign choices of God. It is too costly. God will act against those who do.

- God's concern is for His covenant people and His name. His concern for His people is greater than His concern for any individual leader. The lives of His covenant people are the means through which He intends to carry out His eternal purposes.

- A leader should always know what is in the heart and mind of God for His people. If a leader no longer is hearing the voice of God, he has departed from God and must immediately seek God's face and return to Him as seen in this passage:

But if your heart turns away so that you do not hear, and are drawn away, and worship other gods and serve them, I announce to you today that you shall surely perish; you shall not prolong your days in the land which you cross over the Jordan to go in and possess. I call heaven and earth as witnesses today against you, that I have set before you life and death, blessing and cursing; therefore choose life, that both you and your descendants may live; that you may love the LORD your God, that you may obey His voice, and that you may cling to Him, for He is your life and the length of your days; and that you may dwell in the land which the LORD swore to your fathers, to Abraham, Isaac, and Jacob, to give them. (Deut. 30:17–20)

Heed the warning . . . and choose life!

TWELVE

SAMUEL'S FINAL CHAPTER

Yet they shall be ministers in My sanctuary, as gatekeepers of the house and ministers of the house; they shall slay the burnt offering and the sacrifice for the people, and they shall stand before them to minister to them.

Ezekiel 44:11

OFTEN WHAT A PERSON IS DOING IN THE LAST CHAPTER of his life reveals his life-character! Samuel was standing as leader over a "school of prophets" (see 1 Sam. 19:20). This is the last picture we have of Samuel during his life. He is not only a leader, but he is a leader over the prophets. These were very special people in the lives of the people of God. Little did they know how important leaders were to their spiritual survival. They knew they were special in their midst, but there is no evidence I can see that they paid any particular attention to them. Rather, they continued on in their evil lifestyle, offending God at every turn.

It is a sad day when the people of God take for granted those God may have placed in their midst to keep them close to Him. Samuel was not caught up in the petty politics of Saul and Israel. He was training prophets to walk before God as he walked, so that God's people would always know what was on the mind and heart of God. He was teaching them to worship. The leaders of God's people must never be far from genuine worship in their own lives. The intensity of this relationship would be brought to God's people. Though it is not mentioned in this particular passage, we know that Samuel was always presenting offerings to the Lord—teaching the prophets and leading them in the ways of the Lord. Samuel taught them to worship God.

He was also, I believe, instructing them (in New Testament terms) in prophesying as part of their walk in the Spirit of God. The Spirit's presence was obvious before all in the lives of the prophets (see 1 Sam. 10:5, 6, 10; 19:20). Samuel was "standing as leader over them" (1 Sam. 19:20). I am sensing, and on good grounds, that Samuel was leading them in their relationship to the working of the Spirit in their lives. This was their assignment, and the Spirit never came upon anyone, Old or New Testament, except in relation to an assignment from God. Of all the people in the Bible, Samuel knew God, and knew the implications of the Spirit's working in the life of the prophet. He was a recipient. He therefore could teach the prophets. This is crucial to every believer in our day. The Spirit is given to everyone who believes (see John 7:39; Acts 2:38; 1 Cor. 12:13). Just as Paul did in his letters and in person, Samuel also taught the believers how to "walk in the Spirit" (Gal. 5:16–26; see Rom. 8:4).

Samuel was also teaching them how to walk in holiness before God's people. The priests, who were to teach and lead God's people, were to be holy before the people. The book of Leviticus gives clear and careful instructions for the priests. For instance, they were to offer sacrifices for their sins before they were to help the people with their sins. I am certain that Samuel was instructing the prophets in how they were to be living before the people. As the leaders lived holy lives, the people would also walk in holiness before God, which was what they were supposed to do in their covenant with God. They were to be holy, for their God was holy.

This is so true in our day. We, too, are to be holy, as instructed in 1 Peter 1:13–21:

Gird up the loins of your mind, be sober, and rest your hope fully upon the grace that is to be brought to you at the revelation of Jesus Christ; as obedient children, not conforming yourselves to the former lusts, as in your ignorance; but as He who called you is holy, you also be holy in all your conduct, because it is written, *"Be holy, for I am holy."* And if you call on the Father, who without partiality judges according to each one's work, conduct yourselves throughout the time of your stay here in fear; knowing that you were not redeemed with corruptible things, like silver or gold, from your aimless conduct received by tradition from your fathers, but with the precious blood of Christ, as of a lamb without blemish and without spot. He indeed was foreordained before the foundation of the world, but was manifest in these last times for you who through Him believe in God, who raised Him from the dead and gave Him glory, so that your faith and hope are in God.

Also you must understand, "You are a chosen generation, a royal priesthood, a holy nation, His own special people, that you may proclaim the praises of Him who called you out of darkness into His marvelous light; who once were not a people but are now the people of God, who had not obtained mercy but now have obtained mercy" (1 Peter 2:9–10).

Pastors and other leaders, especially teachers of Bible-study groups, must teach God's people to be holy, for He is holy! In other words, Samuel was leaving God's people with the maximum help so they would not sin against God. There would be no excuse for them if they continued to sin. Their choices would be made with the full knowledge of the truth of God!

REPUTATION

In his last days, Samuel's presence and influence on God's people continued to be affirmed by God. His reputation was as a man of God (1 Sam 9:6, 10), seer (1 Sam 9:9, 11), and prophet (1 Sam. 9:9). He was well-known and well respected. People sought him out in times of crisis. Later David sought Samuel's counsel when Saul, in one of his angry fits, sought to kill him with a spear (1 Sam. 19:9–10). When Saul failed to kill David, David escaped and went to Samuel and told him all Saul was doing (v. 18). Then comes an amazing moment unlike any other in all the Scripture. Saul sent messengers to find and kill David. When they found where David was, all of the messengers saw the prophets prophesying. Samuel was leading them, and "the Spirit of God came upon the messengers of Saul, and they also prophesied" (1 Sam. 19:20). Saul then sent messengers again, "and they prophesied likewise." When he sent them the third time, "they prophesied also" (1 Sam. 19:21).Then Saul also went, and in an amazing moment "the Spirit of God was upon him also, and he went on and prophesied" (v. 23), until he came to where Samuel and David were. There Saul "stripped off his clothes and prophesied before Samuel . . . and lay down naked all that day and all that night" (v. 24). Samuel was obviously God's servant. No one could interfere with this relationship. God has many ways to affirm anyone called, assigned, and faithful to Him. Saul learned this the hard way, and it was before the people of God, so they, too, would tremble before God and before His servant.

What an incredible affirmation: (1) the absolute Sovereignty of God; (2) in the midst of His people; (3) that Samuel was still God's prophet; (4) that God had chosen David; and (5) that God was sovereign over the king, regardless of his spiritual condition. God was present, and God was in full control of everything concerning His people. So open and obvious was this moment that from that moment on, it was said among all the people, "Is Saul also among the prophets?" (1 Sam. 19:24).

What can be learned for our lives today from this moment in Scripture? Several things come to mind, to which we must give close attention:

1. God is always, at all times, intimately aware of and involved in both our lives and the lives of His people. Saul became painfully aware of the nature of God in His total sovereignty, especially when it came to His

servants and His people. Saul could not influence at all any situation for himself, when he touched the people of God. God sees and knows His people, and in the midst of them works His perfect will. There must come a fresh awareness of the absolute sovereignty of God in the midst of His people. Too many in our day are "touching the people of God" for their own purposes. If we are to learn from this moment in the life of Samuel, we must learn that this is extremely dangerous. It is a serious matter to do any harm to God's people. Paul warned some in the church at Corinth saying, "Do you not know that you [the church at Corinth] are the temple of God and that the Spirit of God dwells in you? If anyone defiles [destroys] the temple of God, God will destroy him. For the temple of God is holy, which temple you are" (1 Cor. 3:16–17). Everyone must treat the people of God as holy to God, and therefore sacred to Him. They are a covenant people, and God is very jealous for His name in and through His people.

> **God sees and knows His people, and in the midst of them works His perfect will.**

2. He sovereignly controls all things, even our worst moments, such as Saul's seeking to kill David, God's newly anointed king for His people. Saul never seems to genuinely recognize the nature of the sovereignty of God in the midst of His people. And he would learn in this experience that even when he was at his worst, God would take his worst motives and actions and work them for His glory and good. This is the only time in the Scriptures that God ever did this, but what He did here to Saul and those Saul controlled stunned the people of God. From this act of God, the people spoke of what God did to Saul by exclaiming, "Is Saul also among the prophets?" (1 Sam. 19:24). But the further one proceeds into this life of Samuel, the more there is the frightening awareness of the terrible hardness of heart that sin can bring to God's people, even the chosen leaders. No matter what deep impressions God sought to make on the hearts of His people and the king, they never seemed to "get His message"—repent and return to God and His covenant with them. If they had only turned from their sins, they

would not have been brought back under the captivity of their enemies, especially the Philistines. But once again they refused to obey God.

How sad it is today when God's people do not recognize or respond to the activity of God in the midst of His people, seeking to bring them from their sins to holiness. His people, in His churches, continue in sin to this day. To too large a degree, sin remains unchecked. When this is true, God no longer expresses His power to save a lost world, and situations progressively get worse in the churches. Though there are many churches seeking diligently to do God's will and live holy lives, they seem to be in the minority of the total people of God. Family life and marriages are in a sad condition. Pornography seems to be unchallenged. The world continues to shape God's people. God is never indifferent to sin, in any form, and moves to sanctify His name, in His people, before a watching world. He stated this intention to the people in Ezekiel's day, saying, "I will sanctify My great name, which has been profaned among the nations, which you have profaned in their midst; and the nations shall know that I am the LORD . . . when I am hallowed in you before their eyes" (Ezek. 36:23). To do this, God put His people in seventy years of bondage in Babylon. What could God do in our day? Even more sobering, what *will* He do? If we are to avoid what God did to His people in Samuel's day when they sinned and would not repent—revival is crucial!

3. His mercy spares us because of His covenant with us. I am so glad the very nature of God was revealed as mercy (see Ex. 34:6–7). Mercy means that God chooses to withhold from us what we really deserve because of our sin against Him. But in this very revelation of His nature as mercy, He adds, "by no means clearing the guilty, visiting the iniquity of the fathers upon the children and the children's children to the third and the fourth generation" (Ex. 34:7). At this moment in Samuel's life, God spared His people. But they despised the mercy of the Lord and sinned further, and God's mercy was replaced with jealousy for His name, and He judged them once again.

And He said: "Behold, I make a covenant. Before all your people I will do marvels such as have not been done in all the earth, nor in any nation; and all the people among whom you are shall see the work of the LORD. For it is an awesome thing that I will do with you . . . Take heed to yourself, lest you make a covenant with the inhabitants of the land where you are going, lest it be a snare in your midst. But you shall destroy their altars, break their sacred pillars, and cut down their wooden images (for you shall worship no other god, for the LORD, whose name is Jealous, is a jealous God)." (Ex. 34:10, 12–14)

4. He will make an example of us before everyone if He wants to do so. He is God! He can cause a king to lie naked all day and night before His people. How strange and terrible are the ways of God. Saul, Samuel, and all God's people came to see this in the way He dealt with the king. Naked, all night, before his people. God can do such things to any of His people who do not take seriously the holiness of God and His name. Today it seems as if God's people have lost the *fear of God* and therefore have lost the *fear of sin*. A high view of God brings a high view of sin. A low view of God leads to a low view of sin and carelessness in our covenant with God. I could describe this side of the nature of God clearly, in our day, both in the lives of individuals and in churches, and even ministry groups and denominations: "Do not be deceived, God is not mocked; for whatever a man sows, that he will also reap" (Gal. 6:7).

5. He may give us one more chance to know Him and obey Him even when He knows how hard our hearts are. All through the Bible God reveals Himself as a God of second chances. God does not desire to bring immediate or final judgment when His people sin. He extends His mercy, often for centuries on some nations, giving every opportunity to repent. Occasionally one city does repent, like Nineveh, and God spares them. God expressed His fairness in dealing with sin and repentance in Ezekiel 33:11–16:

Say to them: "As I live," says the Lord GOD, "I have no pleasure in the death of the wicked, but that the wicked turn from his way and live. Turn, turn from your evil ways! For why should you die, O house of Israel?"

Therefore you, O son of man, say to the children of your people: "The righteousness of the righteous man shall not deliver him in the day of his transgression; as for the wickedness of the wicked, he shall not fall because of it in the day that he turns from his wickedness; nor shall the righteous be able to live because of his righteousness in the day that he sins." When I say to the righteous that he shall surely live, but he trusts in his own righteousness and commits iniquity, none of his righteous works shall be remembered; but because of the iniquity that he has committed, he shall die. Again, when I say to the wicked, "You shall surely die," if he turns from his sin and does what is lawful and right, if the wicked restores the pledge, gives back what he has stolen, and walks in the statutes of life without committing iniquity, he shall surely live; he shall not die. None of his sins which he has committed shall be remembered against him; he has done what is lawful and right; he shall surely live.

What a warning, and an encouragement from our loving God, who is not willing that any perish, but all come to repentance—especially His people!

6. Be very careful not to touch God's anointed. Saul was stopped cold by God when he sought to kill David, and God did it uniquely as only He can do. Saul took into his own hands a threat against David, whom God had ordained to replace Saul as king. God would not allow Saul to do this, nor does He ever allow such a thing to happen. If He delays judgment, it should never be read as "It's God's will that I do this!" Don't ever take into your hands the removal of anyone whom God has chosen to lead His people, no matter how logical it may seem to you. Let God alone do this. He will, if He

wants to do it, but you should not try to "play God" and do it for Him. Too many churches today are removing their pastors because they do not suit various individuals in these churches. This is very dangerous. Learn from Samuel's life with Saul.

You should not try to "play God."

7. Your action will not affect God's ultimate purposes in history. Saul's decision to kill David did not affect the purposes of God. It affected only Saul and his life and his family. The sovereignty of God in the midst of His people is very sacred. He will do all that He pleases and all that He purposes. Remember Isaiah 14:24, 27:

> The LORD of hosts has sworn, saying,
> "Surely, as I have thought, so it shall come to pass,
> And as I have purposed, so it shall stand . . .
> For the LORD of hosts has purposed,
> And who will annul it?
> His hand is stretched out,
> And who will turn it back?"

How carefully we must learn the ways of God from His dealing with His people in the Scriptures!

8. God sovereignly releases His Spirit on those whom He wills to do so, in order to fulfill His purposes—in His own time and way. He can place His Spirit on Saul at the beginning of his call, and now at this time, maybe as a reminder to Saul of what used to be and maybe what could have been. God also uniquely did this on Saul's three groups of messengers. He is God, and He can, and will, do as He chooses to do. It is ours to experience Him, and ask Him how we are to respond to what He is doing.

9. When God intervenes, it may be a permanent testimony to Him, such as the woman who poured an alabaster jar of ointment on Jesus:

And when Jesus was in Bethany at the house of Simon the leper, a woman came to Him having an alabaster flask of very costly fragrant oil, and she poured it on His head as He sat at the table. But when His disciples saw it, they were indignant, saying, "Why this waste? For this fragrant oil might have been sold for much and given to the poor." But when Jesus was aware of it, He said to them, "Why do you trouble the woman? For she has done a good work for Me. For you have the poor with you always, but Me you do not have always. For in pouring this fragrant oil on My body, she did it for My burial. Assuredly, I say to you, wherever this gospel is preached in the whole world, what this woman has done will also be told as a memorial to her." (Matt. 26:6–13)

10. God is always revealed and glorified in what He does, especially in the midst of His people. Here God reveals the utter uniqueness of Himself and His ways. God then works in these messengers of Saul, and Saul himself to prophesy.

You may want to meditate further on this moment, until God grants to you a fuller understanding of all He is doing in your life. But this *defining moment* was unique. God may also want to do something unique in your life or church.

GOD'S WAYS ARE NOT OUR WAYS

When God announced, "My ways are not your ways" (see Isa. 55:8–9), this was an understatement! Thus, God permitted Samuel to come before Saul one more time. This time it was to announce Saul's impending death while in battle against the Philistines. Samuel had died (see 1 Sam. 25:1; 28:3). The enemy again came against God's people. This time, however, King Saul could no longer seek counsel from the prophet about whether to go into battle. So his heart instinctively turned to God for himself. "And when Saul inquired of the LORD, the LORD did not answer him, either by dreams or by

210

Urim or by the prophets" (1 Sam. 28:6). So he sought a medium in order to inquire of her. In the process the medium was permitted by God to "bring up Samuel" (1 Sam. 28:11). She did "bring up Samuel," realizing Saul deceived her. God permitted Samuel to confront Saul, but the word from God through even the deceased Samuel once again was not a good word for Saul:

> Then Samuel said: "So why do you ask me, seeing the LORD has departed from you and has become your enemy? And the LORD has done for Himself as He spoke by me. For the LORD has torn the kingdom out of your hand and given it to your neighbor, David. Because you did not obey the voice of the LORD nor execute His fierce wrath upon Amalek, therefore the LORD has done this thing to you this day. Moreover the LORD will also deliver Israel with you into the hand of the Philistines. And tomorrow you and your sons will be with me. The LORD will also deliver the army of Israel into the hand of the Philistines." (1 Sam. 28:16–19)

Oh, the sovereign ways of God! They are His alone to perform. This last encounter with Samuel was *final* for Saul—and for Saul's sons! The sins of the father would come on his sons, even David's closest friend and companion, Jonathan. This tragic end of Saul and his sons is painfully recorded in 1 Samuel 31. The sorrowful lamentation of David for his king, and Jonathan his close friend, is recorded in 2 Samuel 1:17–27. Read it, and weep with David!

ACCOUNTABLE TO GOD ALONE

Some of you may be overseers of organizations, but you are not seeing the blessings of God as you desire. Ezekiel 44:10 and 11 provide a clear picture of the root cause of God's refusing to bless His chosen spiritual leaders: "And the Levites who went far from Me, when Israel went astray, who strayed away from Me after their idols, they shall bear their iniquity. Yet they shall be ministers in My sanctuary, as gatekeepers of the house and ministers of the house; they shall slay the burnt offering and the sacrifice for the people, and they shall stand before them to minister to them."

Now if you learn anything at all it should be that God calls us to Himself—to minister to Him, to be before Him. We read that in 1 Samuel 2:35. I want you to notice how everything in the mind of God relates to your relationship to Him, not merely your activity. Can you be in the middle of the activity but your heart be far from Him? You can. Then the Scripture says, "And they shall not come near Me to minister to Me as priest, nor come near any of My holy things, nor into the Most Holy Place; but they shall bear their shame and their abominations which they have committed" (Ezek. 44:13).

When God finally gives His sentence to the spiritual leaders, He will say, "When the people went astray from Me in their hearts, you did also. You pleased the people and went with them instead of with Me. Now I make a decree, you will not minister to Me." But notice what He says in verse 14: "Nevertheless, I will make them keep charge of the temple, for all its work, and for all that has to be done in it."

In other words, you will be maintaining the organization—making sure that the church is administrated properly—but you will not come near Him. Then He speaks about the second group:

But the priests, the Levites, the sons of Zadok, who kept charge of My sanctuary when the children of Israel went astray from Me, they shall come near Me to minister to Me; and they shall stand before Me to offer to Me the fat and the blood," says the Lord GOD. "They shall enter My sanctuary, and they shall come near My table to minister to Me, and they shall keep My charge. (vv. 15–16)

I did not want to just pass over that. There is a radical difference all through the Scripture between those who started well, were called of God to a relationship with Him, but somewhere in the midst of it all they got caught up with what the people wanted. They adapted and adjusted so they would be one with the people. But in doing so they went astray, with the people, from Him. When a critical moment comes for Him to look for someone to stand before Him, for the land, He will not choose you. And at times you will cry unto Him with all of your heart and there will seem to be no response from God. You will not seem to even get a renewal of your call.

As we examine those priests, there are some questions about our own day. Is it possible to be faithful to the people, but not to God? Can one be a leader among the people, leading an organization and keeping everyone happy, greeted, and even participating in the extensive activities of the church, and be so compromised with God that God chooses not to give such leaders access to Himself, or let him minister to Him?

> **Is it possible to be faithful to the people, but not to God?**

I take Scriptures like this very seriously. You will see the same in the New Testament as the Old Testament. I do not know where God draws the line. But I do not want to try to find out where it is. I do not want to come as close to the edge of the cliff as possible. I want to get as far away from it as possible. I do not want to know where God's line is where one becomes of no use to Him. I want to stay as close to God as I possibly can. And when the people put pressure on me to go their direction, I need to know clearly whether that is the people's direction or God's direction.

I need to know that there will be a difference between following the people and following God. The consequences can be horrendous. So, several years back, I ran this Scripture over my own heart. At times it has been very difficult because people do not always understand when you take a direction that does not please them. You are not there to please them. You are there to serve God. From His presence you serve the people on God's terms, and they will be blessed by God.

It is important that we look again at Ezekiel 44, which reveals the heart of God for a faithful priest and what constituted such a person. Also, it is vital that one *know* the severe consequences for not remaining faithful. This is especially important for our day. The life of God's people again depends on faithfulness, and the eternal purposes of God are affected.

The Scripture indicates that there were two kinds of priests in Ezekiel's day. First, there were "the Levites who went far from Me, when Israel went astray, who strayed away from Me after their idols, they shall bear their iniquity" (Ezek. 44:10). God then adds another stunning announcement to these Levites: "Yet they shall be ministers in My sanctuary, as gatekeepers of the house and ministers of the house; they shall slay the burnt offering and the sacrifice for the people, and they shall stand before them to minister to them" (v. 11). All seems to be fine. However, their assignment was to the people, not to God. They let the people, not God, determine their agenda. They did what the people wanted, but not what God had ordered. In our day we would say they took a poll to see what the people wanted and did that. But they did not stand before God and know what was on His mind and heart, and do that. In other words, they betrayed their initial call from God.

What were the severe consequences of such departing from God? "They shall not come near Me to minister to Me as priest, nor come near any of My holy things, nor into the Most Holy Place; but they shall bear their shame and their abominations which they have committed" (v. 13).

We must take some time to look carefully at this word from God, especially in the light of all that is happening in our day. The spiritual leader was strictly to "minister to God." That is, they were to stand before Him, for His heart and mind, and for His instructions. He was absolutely preeminent in the life of the spiritual leader. God would send spiritual leaders out into the midst of the people, but they were not to take their directions from the people. That would eliminate them from any usefulness before God. They were literally to "minister to" Him. They were to "come near" Him. It was to be in His presence that the spiritual leaders were to stand. This meant that they would come near God's holy things, as in the temple. This was their role before God. And even more significant, they were to come "into the Most Holy Place." Here is the "throne room of God." Only a faithful priest could enter here. It was forbidden by God for any other to enter here.

Those who "went astray, when the people went astray" were now severely limited in their service. They could take care of the people and the house of the Lord. But they could not come near God. What a judgment on His spiritual leaders! Not in the presence of God! Therefore, no word from God. No intimacy with God! And this was to be their calling and assignment—to minister to God.

What a solemn and sacred Scripture for us too! It seems that for some time now the people have cried out to their leaders, "We don't want the restrictions of the Scriptures on us. We want to be free to divorce, to go the ways of the world, and in general, not to trust God anymore." The people have longed for the *gods of this world*—entertainment, success, money, prestige, leaders of the world. We want the marketing ways of the world, the acceptable standards of the world, and the *successes* of the world. We do not want to take time in the presence of God, or study carefully His Word, or spend extended time in prayer. We don't want to walk by faith anymore. And we long for the applause of the media and the world. We offer *pop psychology* for biblical exposition, and exchange true worship for spiritual entertainment. As in the times of Samuel, the people no longer repent, nor do they consider sin serious. They emphasize the love of God, but never the *fear* of God.

But the consequences are the same: There will no longer be a clear sense of the presence of God, and certainly no longer the evidence of the power and activity of God in the midst of His people. The *world* sees no difference in God's people and has marginalized them in the affairs of men. It seems that the *salt* has lost its saltiness, and the *Light* no longer disperses the darkness, and God's people "love to have it so" (Jer. 5:31). Hear this word from the heart of God in Jeremiah 5:30–31, and weep.

THE TRUE SPIRITUAL LEADER

But there was a second group of priests and Levites. These were the ones, in the judgment of God, who "kept charge of [His] sanctuary when the children of Israel went astray from [Him]" (Ezek. 44:15). These were to be very special to God, as Samuel was.

God said an astounding thing of them: "They shall come near Me to minister to Me; and they shall stand before Me to offer to Me the fat and the blood" (Ezek. 44:15). And then God added, "They shall enter My sanctuary, and they shall come near My table to minister to Me, and they shall keep My charge" (v. 16).

These were the priests who stayed in the presence of God, doing His will, and did not follow the demands of the people. When the people no longer wanted to do all that the covenant required, these remained faithful to God. They did not "go astray from God" when the people did. When God's people began to worship other gods, these servants of God stayed true to God. These now were told they could "come near [Him] to minister to [Him]." They could "stand before [Him] to offer to [Him] the fat and the blood [the necessary offerings required by the LORD]" (v. 15). They were also told, "They shall keep My charge" (v. 16). Only God could grant this, and He did. But it was only for those "who did not go astray from [Him] when the people went astray."

Now comes what I consider one of the most significant marks of a true spiritual leader who takes his place before Holy God: "And they shall teach My people the difference between the holy and the unholy, and cause them to discern between the unclean and the clean. In controversy they shall stand as judges, and judge it according to My judgments. They shall keep My laws and My statutes in all My appointed meetings, and they shall hallow My Sabbaths" (Ezek. 44:23–24).

"They shall teach My people the difference between the holy and the unholy." What an assignment! It can be done only by a leader who:

- stays close to the Lord, and therefore knows when the heart and mind of God are stirred because the people are moving away from Him and His holiness.

- stays close to the Word of God. That is, "in [God's] law he meditates day and night" (Ps. 1:2), and he "delights in" God's commandments, judgments, and statutes. He lives out his life in complete obedience to all God has commanded for His people.

- keeps his relationship with the Lord so that the Lord grants him this crucial assignment in the midst of His people. God does not trust this to just anyone, for the future of His people is at stake. As goes the spiritual leader, so go the people.

- knows clearly the difference between the holy and the unholy, the clean and the unclean, and trembles before Holy God. He therefore earnestly, diligently, keeps God's Word in his heart, and lives carefully by it. Then he is able to teach others also. He is especially able to teach his children. And he is able to not only teach but to convince the "elders" concerning the importance in their lives and families of walking faithfully in all the ways of God. Together they tremble before the Lord.

However, if the spiritual leaders depart from God, when the people go away from God, the leaders are never able to teach them God's ways, and the people stray even farther. God had warned them earlier that when the "heart turns away so that you do not hear, and are drawn away, and worship other gods and serve them, I announce to you today that you shall surely perish" (Deut. 30:17–18). This was not an idle threat, but a promise from the covenant. So the leaders who went astray when the people went astray did not teach the people. They no longer were hearing from God, and their hearts were turned away. They began to worship and serve other gods along with the people. This, of course, was fatal.

CONCLUSION

This was what was happening in Samuel's time. Samuel appeared to be the only leader who stayed close to God, and therefore could teach them the difference between the holy and the unholy, and between the clean and the unclean.

How very instructive this is for our day! Too many of God's leaders are merely practicing religion. They take care of the people, make certain the buildings are clean and ready, the bulletin is done, and the Sunday worship services and other meetings are ready for the people. But they may have lost their intimacy with God. Their messages please the people, but they consistently do not receive a word from God. So God's people continue in their sin, sensing all they need to do is be present at the meetings, give a tithe (not all do this anymore), go on a missions trip, and serve in some capacity. But their personal walks with God and their lifestyles in their homes and workplaces go deeper into the ways of the world around them, "serving the gods of this world." They seem completely unaware that they are a covenant people, and that Christ, their Lord, has clear commandments that they are to live by. The leaders are not teaching them the difference between the holy and the unholy or the clean and the unclean. So their lives, their churches, and the nation continue to stray farther and farther from God. God seeks to return them to Himself, but they do not even recognize the one He may send them. They do not realize they are in grave danger of His judgment.

I have always taken very seriously God's call on my life, and my consequent presence in the midst of His people. Anyone who resists God when He is obviously speaking through His servant to His people often is in grave danger. I have seen some awesome things God has done when this occurred, and I literally trembled and wept before God.

We have watched God decide to raise up for Himself "a faithful priest" who would do according to what was in His heart and in His mind (see

1 Sam. 2:35). We have walked with God as He did raise up Samuel, developed and equipped him, and then used him in the midst of His people during many *defining moments* in their lives as a covenant people. Crucial to all God purposed for His people was Samuel, God's spiritual leader. His preeminent work was to know the mind and heart of God, to hear His instructions and obey Him.

But Samuel had to live out his life in the midst of a rebellious and sinful people. The "pressure" is always to stand in the midst of God's people, knowing the mind and heart of God. As long as Samuel walked faithfully with God, He allowed Samuel to come near to Him and minister to Him. But his faithfulness was crucial. He had to be, and remain, a "faithful priest."

Appendix

DEUTERONOMY 28

1: "Now it shall come to pass, if you diligently obey the voice of the LORD your God, to observe carefully all His commandments which I command you today, that the LORD your God will set you high above all nations of the earth.

2: And all these blessings shall come upon you and overtake you, because you obey the voice of the LORD your God:

3: Blessed shall you be in the city, and blessed shall you be in the country.

4: Blessed shall be the fruit of your body, the produce of your ground and the increase of your herds, the increase of your cattle and the offspring of your flocks.

5: Blessed shall be your basket and your kneading bowl.

6: Blessed shall you be when you come in, and blessed shall you be when you go out.

7: The LORD will cause your enemies who rise against you to be defeated before your face; they shall come out against you one way and flee before you seven ways.

8: The LORD will command the blessing on you in your storehouses and in all to which you set your hand, and He will bless you in the land which the LORD your God is giving you.

9: The LORD will establish you as a holy people to Himself, just as

He has sworn to you, if you keep the commandments of the LORD your God and walk in His ways.

10: Then all peoples of the earth shall see that you are called by the name of the LORD, and they shall be afraid of you.

11: And the LORD will grant you plenty of goods, in the fruit of your body, in the increase of your livestock, and in the produce of your ground, in the land of which the LORD swore to your fathers to give you.

12: The LORD will open to you His good treasure, the heavens, to give the rain to your land in its season, and to bless all the work of your hand. You shall lend to many nations, but you shall not borrow.

13: And the LORD will make you the head and not the tail; you shall be above only, and not be beneath, if you heed the commandments of the LORD your God, which I command you today, and are careful to observe them.

14: So you shall not turn aside from any of the words which I command you this day, to the right or the left, to go after other gods to serve them.

15: But it shall come to pass, if you do not obey the voice of the LORD your God, to observe carefully all His commandments and His statutes which I command you today, that all these curses will come upon you and overtake you:

16: Cursed shall you be in the city, and cursed shall you be in the country.

17: Cursed shall be your basket and your kneading bowl.

18: Cursed shall be the fruit of your body and the produce of your land, the increase of your cattle and the offspring of your flocks.

19: Cursed shall you be when you come in, and cursed shall you be when you go out.

20: The LORD will send on you cursing, confusion, and rebuke in all that you set your hand to do, until you are destroyed and until you perish quickly, because of the wickedness of your doings in which you have forsaken Me.

21: The LORD will make the plague cling to you until He has consumed you from the land which you are going to possess.

22: The LORD will strike you with consumption, with fever, with inflammation, with severe burning fever, with the sword, with scorching, and with mildew; they shall pursue you until you perish.

23: And your heavens which are over your head shall be bronze, and the earth which is under you shall be iron.

24: The LORD will change the rain of your land to powder and dust; from the heaven it shall come down on you until you are destroyed.

25: The LORD will cause you to be defeated before your enemies; you shall go out one way against them and flee seven ways before them; and you shall become troublesome to all the kingdoms of the earth.

26: Your carcasses shall be food for all the birds of the air and the beasts of the earth, and no one shall frighten them away.

27: The LORD will strike you with the boils of Egypt, with tumors, with the scab, and with the itch, from which you cannot be healed.

28: The LORD will strike you with madness and blindness and confusion of heart.

29: And you shall grope at noonday, as a blind man gropes in darkness; you shall not prosper in your ways; you shall be only oppressed and plundered continually, and no one shall save you.

30: You shall betroth a wife, but another man shall lie with her; you shall build a house, but you shall not dwell in it; you shall plant a vineyard, but shall not gather its grapes.

31: Your ox shall be slaughtered before your eyes, but you shall not eat of it; your donkey shall be violently taken away from before you, and shall not be restored to you; your sheep shall be given to your enemies, and you shall have no one to rescue them.

32: Your sons and your daughters shall be given to another people, and your eyes shall look and fail with longing for them all day long; and there shall be no strength in your hand.

33: A nation whom you have not known shall eat the fruit of your land and the produce of your labor, and you shall be only oppressed and crushed continually.

34: So you shall be driven mad because of the sight which your eyes see.

35: The LORD will strike you in the knees and on the legs with severe boils which cannot be healed, and from the sole of your foot to the top of your head.

36: The LORD will bring you and the king whom you set over you to a nation which neither you nor your fathers have known, and there you shall serve other gods—wood and stone.

37: And you shall become an astonishment, a proverb, and a byword among all nations where the LORD will drive you.

38: You shall carry much seed out to the field but gather little in, for the locust shall consume it.

39: You shall plant vineyards and tend them, but you shall neither drink of the wine nor gather the grapes; for the worms shall eat them.

40: You shall have olive trees throughout all your territory, but you shall not anoint yourself with the oil; for your olives shall drop off.

41: You shall beget sons and daughters, but they shall not be yours; for they shall go into captivity.

42: Locusts shall consume all your trees and the produce of your land.

43: The alien who is among you shall rise higher and higher above you, and you shall come down lower and lower.

44: He shall lend to you, but you shall not lend to him; he shall be the head, and you shall be the tail.

45: Moreover all these curses shall come upon you and pursue and overtake you, until you are destroyed, because you did not obey the voice of the LORD your God, to keep His commandments and His statutes which He commanded you.

46: And they shall be upon you for a sign and a wonder, and on your descendants forever.

47: Because you did not serve the LORD your God with joy and gladness of heart, for the abundance of everything,

48: therefore you shall serve your enemies, whom the LORD will send against you, in hunger, in thirst, in nakedness, and in need of everything; and He will put a yoke of iron on your neck until He has destroyed you.

49: The LORD will bring a nation against you from afar, from the end of the earth, as swift as the eagle flies, a nation whose language you will not understand,

50: a nation of fierce countenance, which does not respect the elderly nor show favor to the young.

51: And they shall eat the increase of your livestock and the produce of your land, until you are destroyed; they shall not leave you grain or new wine or oil, or the increase of your cattle or the offspring of your flocks, until they have destroyed you.

52: They shall besiege you at all your gates until your high and fortified walls, in which you trust, come down throughout all your land; and they shall besiege you at all your gates throughout all your land which the LORD your God has given you.

53: You shall eat the fruit of your own body, the flesh of your sons and your daughters whom the LORD your God has given you, in the siege and desperate straits in which your enemy shall distress you.

54: The sensitive and very refined man among you will be hostile

toward his brother, toward the wife of his bosom, and toward the rest of his children whom he leaves behind,

55: so that he will not give any of them the flesh of his children whom he will eat, because he has nothing left in the siege and desperate straits in which your enemy shall distress you at all your gates.

56: The tender and delicate woman among you, who would not venture to set the sole of her foot on the ground because of her delicateness and sensitivity, will refuse to the husband of her bosom, and to her son and her daughter,

57: her placenta which comes out from between her feet and her children whom she bears; for she will eat them secretly for lack of everything in the siege and desperate straits in which your enemy shall distress you at all your gates.

58: If you do not carefully observe all the words of this law that are written in this book, that you may fear this glorious and awesome name, THE LORD YOUR GOD,

59: then the LORD will bring upon you and your descendants extraordinary plagues—great and prolonged plagues—and serious and prolonged sicknesses.

60: Moreover He will bring back on you all the diseases of Egypt, of which you were afraid, and they shall cling to you.

61: Also every sickness and every plague, which is not written in this Book of the Law, will the LORD bring upon you until you are destroyed.

62: You shall be left few in number, whereas you were as the stars of heaven in multitude, because you would not obey the voice of the LORD your God.

63: And it shall be, that just as the LORD rejoiced over you to do you good and multiply you, so the LORD will rejoice over you to destroy you and bring you to nothing; and you shall be plucked from off the land which you go to possess.

64: Then the LORD will scatter you among all peoples, from one end of the earth to the other, and there you shall serve other gods, which neither you nor your fathers have known—wood and stone.

65: And among those nations you shall find no rest, nor shall the sole of your foot have a resting place; but there the LORD will give you a trembling heart, failing eyes, and anguish of soul.

66: Your life shall hang in doubt before you; you shall fear day and night, and have no assurance of life.

67: In the morning you shall say, 'Oh, that it were evening!' And at evening you shall say, 'Oh, that it were morning!' because of the fear which terrifies your heart, and because of the sight which your eyes see.

68: And the LORD will take you back to Egypt in ships, by the way of which I said to you, 'You shall never see it again.' And there you shall be offered for sale to your enemies as male and female slaves, but no one will buy you."

LEVITICUS 26

1: "'You shall not make idols for yourselves;
   neither a carved image nor a sacred pillar shall you rear up for yourselves;
   nor shall you set up an engraved stone in your land, to bow down to it;
   for I am the LORD your God.

2: You shall keep My Sabbaths and reverence My sanctuary:
   I am the LORD.

3: If you walk in My statutes and keep My commandments, and perform them,

4: then I will give you rain in its season, the land shall yield its produce, and the trees of the field shall yield their fruit.

5: Your threshing shall last till the time of vintage, and the vintage shall last till the time of sowing;

you shall eat your bread to the full, and dwell in your land safely.

6: I will give peace in the land, and you shall lie down, and none will make you afraid;

I will rid the land of evil beasts,

and the sword will not go through your land.

7: You will chase your enemies, and they shall fall by the sword before you.

8: Five of you shall chase a hundred, and a hundred of you shall put ten thousand to flight;

your enemies shall fall by the sword before you.

9: For I will look on you favorably and make you fruitful, multiply you and confirm My covenant with you.

10: You shall eat the old harvest, and clear out the old because of the new.

11: I will set My tabernacle among you, and My soul shall not abhor you.

12: I will walk among you and be your God, and you shall be My people.

13: I am the LORD your God, who brought you out of the land of Egypt, that you should not be their slaves;

I have broken the bands of your yoke and made you walk upright.

14: But if you do not obey Me, and do not observe all these commandments,

15: and if you despise My statutes, or if your soul abhors My judgments, so that you do not perform all My commandments, but break My covenant,

16: I also will do this to you:

I will even appoint terror over you, wasting disease and fever which shall consume the eyes and cause sorrow of heart.

And you shall sow your seed in vain, for your enemies shall eat it.

17: I will set My face against you, and you shall be defeated by your enemies.

Those who hate you shall reign over you, and you shall flee when no one pursues you.

18: And after all this, if you do not obey Me, then I will punish you seven times more for your sins.

19: I will break the pride of your power;

I will make your heavens like iron and your earth like bronze.

20: And your strength shall be spent in vain;

for your land shall not yield its produce, nor shall the trees of the land yield their fruit.

21: Then, if you walk contrary to Me, and are not willing to obey Me, I will bring on you seven times more plagues, according to your sins.

22: I will also send wild beasts among you, which shall rob you of your children, destroy your livestock, and make you few in number; and your highways shall be desolate.

23: And if by these things you are not reformed by Me, but walk contrary to Me,

24: then I also will walk contrary to you, and I will punish you yet seven times for your sins.

25: And I will bring a sword against you that will execute the vengeance of the covenant;

when you are gathered together within your cities I will send pestilence among you;

and you shall be delivered into the hand of the enemy.

26: When I have cut off your supply of bread, ten women shall bake your bread in one oven, and they shall bring back your bread by weight, and you shall eat and not be satisfied.

27: And after all this, if you do not obey Me, but walk contrary to Me,

28: then I also will walk contrary to you in fury;

and I, even I, will chastise you seven times for your sins.

29: You shall eat the flesh of your sons, and you shall eat the flesh of your daughters.

30: I will destroy your high places, cut down your incense altars, and cast your carcasses on the lifeless forms of your idols;
and My soul shall abhor you.

31: I will lay your cities waste and bring your sanctuaries to desolation, and I will not smell the fragrance of your sweet aromas.

32: I will bring the land to desolation, and your enemies who dwell in it shall be astonished at it.

33: I will scatter you among the nations and draw out a sword after you;
your land shall be desolate and your cities waste.

34: Then the land shall enjoy its sabbaths as long as it lies desolate and you are in your enemies' land;
then the land shall rest and enjoy its sabbaths.

35: As long as it lies desolate it shall rest—
for the time it did not rest on your sabbaths when you dwelt in it.

36: And as for those of you who are left, I will send faintness into their hearts in the lands of their enemies;
the sound of a shaken leaf shall cause them to flee;
they shall flee as though fleeing from a sword, and they shall fall when no one pursues.

37: They shall stumble over one another, as it were before a sword, when no one pursues;
and you shall have no power to stand before your enemies.

38: You shall perish among the nations, and the land of your enemies shall eat you up.

39: And those of you who are left shall waste away in their iniquity in your enemies' lands;
also in their fathers' iniquities, which are with them, they shall waste away.

40: But if they confess their iniquity and the iniquity of their fathers, with their unfaithfulness in which they were unfaithful to Me, and that they also have walked contrary to Me,

41: and that I also have walked contrary to them and have brought them into the land of their enemies;
    if their uncircumcised hearts are humbled, and they accept their guilt—

42: then I will remember My covenant with Jacob, and My covenant with Isaac and My covenant with Abraham I will remember;
    I will remember the land.

43: The land also shall be left empty by them, and will enjoy its sabbaths while it lies desolate without them;
    they will accept their guilt, because they despised My judgments and because their soul abhorred My statutes.

44: Yet for all that, when they are in the land of their enemies, I will not cast them away, nor shall I abhor them, to utterly destroy them and break My covenant with them;
    for I am the LORD their God.

45: But for their sake I will remember the covenant of their ancestors, whom I brought out of the land of Egypt in the sight of the nations, that I might be their God:
    I am the LORD.'"

46: These are the statutes and judgments and laws which the LORD made between Himself and the children of Israel on Mount Sinai by the hand of Moses.

NOTES

CHAPTER 2: Samuel Ministered to the Lord
1. Brian Edwards, *Revival: A People Saturated with God* (Durham, England: Evangelical Press, 1990), 115.

CHAPTER 3: A Godly Father and Mother
1. See my book, *Experiencing God Together* (Nashville: Broadman and Holman, 202).

CHAPTER 7: The Spirit of the Lord Came
1. See such guidance in my book, *Fresh Encounter: God's Pattern for Revival and Spiritual Awakening* (Nashville: LifeWay Press, 1993).

CHAPTER 8: Israel Demands a King
1. See Henry and Richard Blackaby, *Spiritual Leadership: Leading People on to God's Agenda* (Nashville: Broadman and Holman, 2001).

CHAPTER 11: God Chooses His King
1. See Henry and Richard Blackaby, *Hearing God's Voice* (Nashville: Broadman and Holman, 2002).

ABOUT THE AUTHOR

HENRY T. BLACKABY HAS SPENT HIS LIFE IN MINISTRY. He has served as a music director, Christian education director, and senior pastor in churches in California and Canada; his first church assignment was in 1958. During his local church ministry, Dr. Blackaby became a college president, a missionary, and later an executive in Southern Baptist Convention life.

Dr. Blackaby formerly served on staff at the North American Mission Board in Alpharetta, Georgia, as Special Assistant to the President. Through the office of Revival and Spiritual Awakening of the Southern Baptist Convention, he provided leadership to thousands of pastors and laymen across North America. He also served concurrently as Special Assistant to the Presidents of the International Mission Board and LifeWay Christian Resources for global revival.

In the early '90s, Henry Blackaby became one of North America's best-selling Christian authors, committing the rest of his life to helping people know and experience God.

The author of more than a dozen books, Dr. Blackaby is a graduate of the University of British Columbia, Vancouver, Canada. He has completed his Th.M. degree from Golden Gate Baptist Theological Seminary. He has also received four honorary doctorate degrees.

Henry Blackaby and his wife, Marilynn, have five married children, all serving in Christian ministry. They are also blessed with thirteen grandchildren. Henry is now serving as the president of Henry Blackaby Ministries.

HENRY BLACKABY MINISTRIES

Henry Blackaby Ministries exists to help people experience a life-changing relationship with God that dynamically affects their home, church, and business through a message of revival and spiritual awakening.

We seek to help people experience God through preaching, teaching, conference speaking, leadership training, the production and presentation of ministry materials, and various media outlets, including radio and the Internet.

For further information about Henry Blackaby Ministries, please contact:

Henry Blackaby Ministries
P.O. Box 161228
Atlanta, GA 30321
hbm@henryblackaby.com
www.henryblackaby.com

ACKNOWLEDGMENTS

SPECIAL THANKS to Kerry Skinner, who spent countless hours editing and formatting this book. Also to Connie Yancey, Lois Quattlebaum, and Jan Robertson for checking the manuscript. To my daughter, Carrie Blackaby Webb, who helped in typing four of the chapters while we were visiting her and her family in Germany. And to my wife, Marilynn, for her incredible patience, understanding, and encouragement.

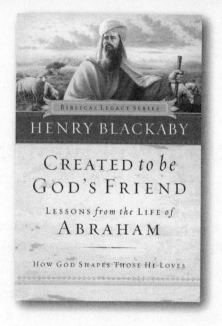

God called Abraham to be His friend. Henry Blackaby uses the example set by Abraham to show how God uses difficult events, traumatic circumstances, and trying life experiences to lead us to spiritual maturity. Readers will learn how God interacts with His people to transform them into men and women He can call friends. From the first time we respond to God's Spirit in our lives through the choices that help us develop a worthy character, Abraham's story shows us how we can be transformed and become friends of God.

ISBN: 0-7852-6982-7

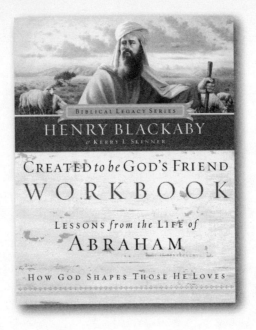

Using the life of Abraham as his palette, bestselling author Henry T. Blackaby shows how God shapes and sculpts men and women so that eventually they can become His friend. This workbook helps readers apply the truths of *Created to Be God's Friend*, understanding how God uses difficult events, traumatic circumstances, and trying life experiences to lead us into spiritual maturity.

ISBN 0-7852-6758-1